Your Life

How to Turn Everyday Activities into Spiritually Rewarding Experiences

by

Dr. Kathleen A. Hall

ISBN 0-9745427-8-4

Library of Congress Control Number 2003111921.

www.alteryourlife.com

Printed in the United States
First Edition
9 8 7 6 5 4 3 2 1

Table of Contents

•INTRODUCTION•
An Invitation · 11

•CHAPTER ONE•
Awareness · 17

•CHAPTER TWO•
The Power of Surrender · 49

Acknowledgments

BLESSING IS THE WORD that best describes the process of writing this book. The fabric of my life has been woven together with wise and loving teachers, gifted healers, friends and family. Thank you all for sharing this journey.

Thank you Cynthia Cohen. You came into my life as a guiding light that has led me on an adventure greater than I had imagined. Your searing insight, focus, persistence and love made this book possible. You are my "shero" and my friend.

Thank you Rick Roberts, the editor who inspired me to write this particular book for Harriet. Your seasoned skill challenged me and helped me flesh out the book and gave me the sacred gift of Harriet. You did survive "Hell Week at Camp Estrogen" and I think you are better for it. I know I am. You are a genius my friend.

Thank you Donna Godzisz. You are my angel of God. You are my confidant, an ingenious source of wisdom and love along with being my literary assistant. You are my friend who spent innumerable hours typing and sharing egg and cheese sandwiches as we wrote while watching the sun rise at Waffle House. Your energy, loyalty and dedication continually inspires and encourages me.

Thank you to my friends. Pamela Hayling Hoffman, my constant source of love, loyalty, and encouragement. I love you. Donna Andrews, a gift of support and guidance in many hours of darkness. I love you.

Thank you to my team at Alter Your Life; you are the wind beneath my wings. We are family—I love you.

Thank you to the people who have believed in my dream and blessed me with resources to make it come true, my friends David Stovall, Eddie Hood, and Rich White.

Thank you to my spiritual teachers and mentors, who are too many to name you all. To name a few, Dr. Bill Mallard, Dr. Roberta Bondi, Dr. Sally Purvis, Dr. John Kloepfer, President Jimmy Carter, Bishop Desmond Tutu, Arun Gandhi, the Dalai Lama, Thich Nhat Hanh, Wong Loh Sin See, and all the saints of the Church who constantly inspire me and give me courage.

Thank you to the gifted healers that have helped heal my heart and soul, Dr. Pat Malone, Dr. Carol Holzhalb, and Wendy Palmer Patterson.

Thank you to my beautiful mother, Mary Lee Clennan who has a voice like an angel, who taught me to laugh, dream, listen to my inner voice, write, and love.

Thank you to my father, Dale F. Hall, who taught me the value of hard work, forgiveness, and the infinite possibilities created when you take risks.

Thank you to my family—Jon, Jeffrey, Pamela, Patricia, Candice, and Will—for our difficult lives fraught with suffering, joy and hope. There's light at the end of the tunnel.

Thank you Pat Walsh, Capitol Area Mosaic and my kids who taught me about real economic poverty, spiritual wealth and that infinite possibilities are everywhere.

Thank you to Oak Haven—my farm, my Avalon, my Camelot, my Walden Pond all in one. Thank you to the animals that have been my most profound teachers. Thank you Secret, Reba and all of the sacred horses that have taught me invaluable lessons about power, death, fear and mothering. I shall be eternally grateful—I love you.

I love you Lady, Holly, Lucy, and Abbey, my angel dogs who are now with the angels. Thank you to all of my dogs for teaching me about love, playfulness, loyalty and wisdom. A special thank you to Chloe for never leaving my side through my depression, my dissertation, writing this book, and life.

Thank you JC Cowart. You have been a constant source of strength. You are a dying breed of cowboy and farmer. You have been my great teacher about the land, animals, the weather and life.

Thank you to my patients and clients who have been my teachers, mentors and family. A special thank you to the Cardiac-Pulmonary Wellness Group: Shirlene, Dick, Ilone, Nancy, Gail, Wally, Helen, Jane, Lucille, Catherine, Roy, Emily, and you unnamed, but you know who you are. I love you and am eternally grateful.

Thank you my children Brittany and Elizabeth. Brittany, you have always been a source of healing for me, many years before you became a physician. You live and breathe compassion, forgiveness and love. Elizabeth, you have always been a source of passionate love, intuition and creativity. You have been my mirror, my darling, and I am eternally grateful. If I have contributed anything to the healing of this planet in my life, I believe it is the gift of these two children.

Thank you my darling Jim, for 30 years you have been my partner, cheerleader, advisor, and lover. Very few have committed the time and passion to be an amazing husband and father. You have always believed in me. I loved you the first moment I looked into your eyes at the Medical Center and I always will.

I am grateful Holy One—Divine Presence, God Creator of all life—I live every moment aware of your presence, guidance, protection and love. I live my life to be one with you in the sacred process of co-creation. I love you.

Alter Your Life

The

Invitation

THE THEMES THAT RULE OUR LIVES today are, "I just don't have time" and "I'm exhausted." We are overbooked, overworked and overwhelmed. Just getting done what must be done fills our days. The notion of finding a precious hour or two for spiritual pursuits or studying with a spiritual guide or entering a more formal program to soothe our aching souls is simply out of the question. This book is an alternative. It offers you opportunities to turn everyday activities into spiritually rewarding experiences. Its objective is to give the average, busy person the means to awaken their personal spirituality and bring meaning into their lives.

You can do this in a manner that requires no doctrine, no memorization of a new vocabulary, no trekking off to distant holy lands. It does not require you to change your job, your lifestyle or transplant your personality. It doesn't even require any additional time. Sound too good to be true?

Listen: your spirituality is as much a part of you as your emotional and physical being. This is difficult for many of us to understand because society doesn't even teach it; our institutions and cultural traditions don't reveal it. We often feel spiritually untrained, spiritually naïve. As a result, spirituality seems to be something extraordinary, something otherworldly, out of reach, not of us, not a natural part of our existence. For many, spirituality is something that can only be properly addressed through rigorous religious training.

Yet the great religious traditions have always suggested that the finest spiritual moments are available in the common, ordinary, mundane tasks of living. Discovering these precious moments for yourself is the point of this book. Anyone can find them. They are available to you everyday. Practicing them is easy and the remarkable thing is that it is their smallness and simplicity which holds the promise for substantial change in your life, major transformation. It simply begins by seeing the world not just in terms of physical activity and emotional impact, but also in terms of spiritual fulfillment. You have this capacity. We hope this book will be a guide to developing that capacity.

Why should you work on developing your spirituality? True happiness is based on self knowledge, balance, freedom, connection. Happiness today is erroneously seen as the collection of wealth, beauty, or power. In a society driven by a pop culture with lofty benchmarks of athletic prowess, beauty and accumulation of wealth, we must ask ourselves how happy are we really? How many *happy* people, including yourself, do you really know?

By happiness I mean experiencing a meaningful and intentional life. What is missing in your life is not more stuff, or a new diet, or any form of physical accumulation. What is missing for many of us is the ability to see life in spiritual terms, understanding the essence of spirituality, or grasping the true meaning of life. This book creates a path for you to discover the spirituality in your everyday activities and responsibilities. It is about developing practices that will allow you to explore spirituality in every aspect of your existence. The task is simple, the task is at hand. The rewards are extraordinary. Let's begin.

•CHAPTER ONE•

Awareness:
Extracting the Extraordinary from the Ordinary

I

N 1994, I cleaned the girl's bathroom at North Atlanta High School. It wasn't something I had planned to do.

It had been an unusually busy day for me. I was racing from a business meeting to get to my daughter's basketball playoff game. It was dinner time and I had worked through lunch. I was exhausted, hungry, and very late. As I flew up into the stands a buzzer rang signaling the end of the first quarter. My daughter had already scored eight points and the game was tied. I sat down by my husband, but immediately realized I just had to go to the bathroom before the game started again. I jumped up, kissed him, and told him I'd be right back.

I raced down the bleachers with my high heels clicking and my coat falling from my shoulders. I only had a few minutes to get to the women's room and back to watch one of the last basketball games of my daughter's high school career. She was a senior and quite an accomplished guard.

Preoccupied, I threw open the bathroom door and rushed in only to be stopped in my tracks. It was like being hit between the eyes. Before me stood one of the most disgusting scenes I had ever encountered. The restroom was awash in filth; the smell was so bad I gagged. It reeked of urine, feces, and old blood. The mirrors were smattered with obscene graffiti. The sinks were filled with used paper towels, hair, toilet paper, and pooled brown water. The floors were covered with used toilet paper; used sanitary pads had been thrown around everywhere. The toilets had not been flushed in who knows how long and were filled with excrement. It was a scene that is still disturbingly clear in my memory.

Rage followed my initial moments of disgust. I was indignant and appalled and filled with judgment. My thoughts went something like this: "Look at how low human nature can go. It's disgusting for any human being to sink to this level of decadence—let alone in my daughter's school. A public school cannot look like this. Who allows it? This is simply uncivilized. Worse, I cannot believe that I allow my children to go to a school like this."

Then an even darker side of myself crept in. This is what happens when people don't have anything, I thought. This is what happens when the poor come into a beautiful facility like this. They destroy it. They trash it and have no respect for this school or for themselves.

In that exact moment, at the height of my rage, as my heart was racing and my blood pressure was pounding, when the anguish and judgment were most monumental, I just stopped. I realized everything I thought and felt was wrong. My thoughts stopped, my breathing slowed down. An amazing stillness and presence overcame me. I remembered a particular story told to me by my friend Arun Gandhi, the grandson of Mahatma Gandhi. It was a scene that also appeared in the movie. Mahatma Gandhi was reminding his wife that it was her turn to clean the latrine at the ashram at Durban, South Africa. In this particular scene, Gandhi is firmly scolding his wife for not wanting to clean the latrines when it was her turn on the schedule. Gandhi's wife thinks it is below her to clean the latrines, although everyone that lived at the ashram had to take their turn at every task. Gandhi believed that full participation by every human, no matter what their status, brought about an act of humility. Gandhi believed that it was fundamental to holiness and social justice that the most mundane and common activities be shared by all persons equally. He taught that simple actions create humility in a person and thus are an essential lesson on their spiritual journey.

I saw the cleaning closet on my left. I walked over to it, opened the door, and found the cleaning supplies stored inside. I took off my cashmere coat and hung it on the closet door. I rolled up the sleeves to my suit, took a deep breath, and prayed that I could make it through this experience. I prayed to be made better in some way because of it. I started with the floors. As I cleaned up each piece of disgusting trash, I prayed for compassion and understanding. As I cleaned each sink, I prayed for non-judgment and serenity. As I began on the toilets, I prayed to stay centered and strong as the stench enveloped me. Forty-five minutes later, that bathroom sparkled. As I closed the supply closet and picked up my coat, I felt like a very different person than the person who entered that bathroom a short time earlier. I learned that my judgment and anger separated me from an experience that could transform my life. I had discovered that a bathroom filled with the filth of others was a classroom for me. There are people whose job it is to clean bathrooms everyday and I now have a better understanding of these individuals and a great reverence for their courage, perseverance and humility.

I walked back up to my husband in the bleachers and sat down. He thought I had been at the concession stand, or perhaps talking to another parent. I just nodded, smiled, and said nothing. In the second half of the game, my husband leaned over to me and whispered in my ear, "Honey, I smell Clorox. It's strong. Can you smell it, too?" I smiled and answered, "Yes, dear." I said a silent prayer of thanks to Mahatma Gandhi for opening one of many doors that would transform my life.

Everyday events, sometimes the most unlikely ones, are avenues to soulful experiences. Everyday is filled with an abundance of such opportunities; every second is filled with a possibility of change. Did you take a shower today? Eat breakfast? Drive to work? These are all potential spiritual moments.

I WAS WITH MY YOUNGER DAUGHTER one evening on the way to the grocery store. The girls and my husband were hungry, so we were in a hurry. Out of nowhere, a large object appeared in the middle of the road. I slammed on my brakes. As the car slid sideways I tried to make out what was in the road. As the car finally came to a stop I realized it was a large dog. It apparently had been hit by a car and left behind.

I have had a practice for many years now of always stopping when there are dead animals on a road, moving them back to the side of the road, and giving them back to the earth. I do this as an act of reverent respect for all creatures. It continually reminds me that these creatures are sacred and I am responsible for their care and protection. I cannot stand the thought of a dead animal being disrespectfully hit again and again by automobiles.

It was busy on the road. And I was afraid that other cars would hit this dog. I turned the car around and drove beside the dog. I stopped and pushed on my emergency flashers. The poor dog was dead and so precious. I grabbed her two back legs and gently pulled her off to the side of the road. I then pulled her over to the grassy area and squatted beside her.

I took a deep breath and looked back to the car. My daughter was gazing out the window at me, but she did not leave the car. After saying a prayer over the dog I returned to the car. I opened the trunk, pulled out some paper towels and cleaned off my hands. I got in the car and we drove off in silence toward the grocery store. A few minutes later, the silence was broken. My daughter reached over and put her hand over my hand on the gear shift. She tenderly looked at me with teary eyes and said, "You know mom, I just can't do that yet. But I will be able to someday." I smiled and thought to myself: She knows.

How do we find the spiritual moments in our everyday activities? The process is composed of three simple practices: *awareness*, *choice*, and *intention*. We begin by cultivating awareness. We become aware of where we are, what we are thinking, what we are doing. Many people don't practice awareness because the more aware you become, the more engaged you are with the world around you. Though it is challenging, awareness is available to each of us. There is no longer room for pretending you can't hear, see, or smell the world around you.

When you practice awareness, the second part of the process is *choice*. As you develop your awareness, you bring a new light into everything you do. You see and experience things differently. You realize that you don't have to live in a pattern of habituation. In every single thing you do you are choosing a direction. Your life is a product of your choices.

The final stage of the process is living and responding with *intention*. It is essential to know the intention of your life. Who do you want to be? What do you want in your career? Who do want to share your life with? Your intentions lead you to your goals, your dreams, and your aspirations. Embracing awareness, choice, and intention, your life becomes a kaleidoscope of possibilities.

Why should we change the way we are living in the world? Why would I clean a public bathroom? Why would I pick a dead dog up out of the road? Why should we bother to see the world in a spiritual way? Is it worth the effort? I promise you this: in the accumulation of seconds that create these moments of awareness, intentional response can create a lifetime of joy. Our response to the everyday activities of our life can create immeasurable peace of mind. It is precisely these small things that create the avenues to the most fundamental changes within ourselves. God—as they say—is in the details.

Why is this so hard for us to grasp? Perhaps because we live in a world where bigger, faster, and first are best. I choose the philosophy that suggests the smallest and the simplest things hold the greatest potential for transformation. What a wonderful surprise to discover that exercising, washing the dishes, and watching the evening news can change your life.

I REMEMBER WATCHING MOTHER TERESA being interviewed by a CNN correspondent once. He was awed at the idea that Mother Teresa had to date picked up some 30,000 sick and dying off the streets of Calcutta. This correspondent reverently looked into Mother Teresa's eyes and asked her, "How can you not get overwhelmed when you deal with so many sick and dying bodies? You have cared for thousands and thousands of dying people personally. How can you continually do this?"

Mother Teresa said, "The answer is simple, my son. I am with one soul at a time. I am fully present with the person I am with. I imagine that theirs is the face of Christ I am looking into. I never think about yesterday, an hour from now, or tomorrow when I look into their eyes. It is never 30,000 people; it is one person at a time."

Her answer changed my life. We can get overwhelmed trying to do good in the world. How many acts of kindness or charities can we be involved in to help the less fortunate? Heed the words of Mother Teresa, do it one person at a time, one task at a time.

I was a student chaplain at St. Joseph's Hospital many years ago. This institution deals with a number of critical care patients. It is an intense experience to immerse oneself in the spiritual and physical needs of these individuals. I remember one particularly overwhelming day. A woman I had become very attached to had just died of a heart attack. We had disconnected a dying teen from a respirator and harvested her organs for transplant. And a thirteen-year-old had committed suicide. I was confused about God, my faith, my life, and many other things. I remembered the plaque hanging over my desk that had been given to me by a friend who was a chaplain as well. It reads: "We can do no great things, only small things with great love." That quote is from Mother Teresa. It helped me then. And I continue to repeat it every day of my life. It keeps me humble and fills me with joy.

It's now time to explore your day: To find how routine activities—not how extraordinary events—hold the potential to become spiritually rewarding experiences for you.

Waking Up

"If every day is an awakening, you will never grow old. You will just keep growing."
—GAIL SHEEHY

---

*D*OES THIS SOUND LIKE YOU? The clock radio blasts: "I can't get no satisfaction…" You reach over and slap the alarm button, and reluctantly swing your feet to the floor. Perhaps your partner or spouse is already in the shower. Maybe the cat is complaining that breakfast is overdue. You're not sure what day it is.

Not getting satisfaction could very well be the theme song of modern culture. Many of our lives have turned into a series of programmed habits, if not downright desperation. Many of us feel like victims of our own lives.

How do you change this? The three steps we discussed earlier—awareness, choice, and intention—can be applied to all our daily activities right from the moment we awake. That's how to start a more meaningful life: Start with how you wake up in the morning.

The sleep state is similar to being in our mother's womb: dark, peaceful, warm, connected. Emerging from sleep, there-fore, can be seen as the birth process. If you think about wak-ing up as just another routine matter, it becomes stale, old, common, and usual. When you experience waking up as a metaphor for birth, you begin to think of it with new hope, promise and purpose.

Awareness

AS YOU WAKE UP in the morning do not jump out of bed. Pause. The first moment of each day is a moment of awareness. This is a time of exploration. Choose a kind and gentle way to wake up. There are so many options for waking devices, we no longer have to rely on jolting alarms. We don't want to shock our bodies awake with an adrenaline release. Instead try something that wakes you with a soft light or gentle nature sounds.

Breathe: inhale, exhale. It may seem simple, but your breath has critical physical and spiritual implications. In most languages, there is only one word for breath and spirit. In Hindu, *prana*. In Hebrew, *ruah*. In Latin, *pneuma*. In English, however, breath and spirit are two separate words. When your breath has meaning on every level—physical, spiritual, and emotional—you develop reverent respect for this process. Awareness of the breath is a pivotal step to the holy. As you wake and are aware of your breath be, aware of the mind-body connection. Breath is the source of nourishment for our vital organs: brain, heart, liver. You must breathe to survive.

Do a body scan. This is a process of examining your body. How do you feel? Do you have any pains? A headache? Do you have a giggly feeling in your stomach? Start from the top of your head down to your toes. Be grateful for your body. Imagine white light, energy, a color, your favorite music, or water moving down your body. Pick the medium you identify with most to flow through your body. Thank your brain, spinal column, your brainstem for orchestrating the function of your body. Tell your eyes thank you for all that you've witnessed and seen. Tell your ears thank you for all the I-loveyou's you've heard. Continue this process, acknowledging, and showing gratitude for every organ and system of your body.

We know that there is intelligence in every cell of the body. With this body scan you are telling each of these cells that you are grateful for their daily functioning. According to the latest medical studies, communicating with your body causes real chemical changes that create a healing response in your body.

Awakening Moments

MOST GREAT SPIRITUAL TRADITIONS contain moments of awakening. We find it with Mohammad in Islam, Benedict in Christianity, Mary Baker Eddy of Christian Science, John Wesley of Methodism, and of course, the Buddha.

One of the great stories of all time about awakening is in the Buddhist tradition. The story describes the scene of Buddha's death. In the last moments of Buddha's life, he was surrounded by his disciples. They began to ask him, "Holy One, what last words of wisdom would you leave with us? After the many years of teachings and discourse, what is the most important final message you can leave with your devout followers?" At the final moment of his life, Buddha opened his eyes, took his last breath, smiled, and said, "Wake up."

The Shower

---

*"If there is magic on this planet,
it is contained in water."*
—LOREN EISELEY

ATER BY ITS NATURE is invitational. It mesmerizes us. Water invites possibility and sends us deeper into ourselves. There is a sensual, sexual freedom associated with water. Most of us shower in the morning. And by changing our perspective on this habit, it can take on a new sense of adventure. This experience can become a source of power and connection with nature and yourself.

There is no mystery why water is so significant to us. We are mostly water, about 75 percent. Brain tissue consists of 85 percent water. Our blood is 94 percent water. Even teeth are composed of 5 percent water. Water is alive, filled with oxygen and minerals. We are formed in the moving water of our mother's womb. Your interaction with water is your body coming home to itself. There is an inextricable bond with our bodies and water.

Water in the Sacred

NO ORDINARY ELEMENT has received more attention in spiritual practice than water. Water rituals are used in purification. Water symbolizes beginnings, new life, cleansing. The spiritual power of water is the power of invigoration, rebirth, and fresh starts.

Most religions and spiritualities have a ritual or ceremony engaging water. There is the Muslim *wudu*: a ritual washing or cleansing that prepares the mind, body, and spirit for prayer, meals, and countless other times throughout the day. The Cherokee perform a forgiveness ritual that involves going to the ocean, a river, or other moving body of water and pouring water over oneself seven times to carry away guilt or bad memories. In Christianity, baptism is a sacramental water ritual that initiates individuals into the body of the faithful. The water of the Ganges and other sacred rivers in India are vital to prayer, blessing, healing, and dying rituals of the Hindu faith. Buddhism uses water in worship and considers rivers and lakes sacred and holy. Aboriginal peoples believed that the most holy water of all comes from movement: the water of rivers, waterfalls, springs. The religions and belief systems of the world show us that there is power, potential and promise in the movement of water. Then there is the mythical Fountain of Youth with its waters promising eternal life. With this in mind, you have the opportunity to experience your morning shower like a rain shower from the Divine.

Power Shower

WATER IS THE ULTIMATE POWER. Imagine the power and velocity of rain in your morning shower pelting down on your body, stimulating and invigorating, adding new life to your day. The movement of the water is critical in the morning because it transports you from labile sleep into the rhythm of the day. This simple act of awareness can shift this numbing daily habit into an exciting and enriching experience. You can transform a mundane ritual like showering into beginning your day with something life-giving.

There is energy in water. You absorb the energy of the shower. Moving water is powerful. Experience your shower as Niagara Falls. There is a vibration in water, a frequency that energizes and invigorates.

The shower is your time. Your shower is the morning rain. Your shower is the beginning of the daily cycle of your life. Remember the Herbal Essence shampoo commercials? The excited woman is washing her hair and screaming out loud. Her seductive screams in the television ad sound orgasmic. What a shower!

Imagine: waterfalls, torrents of rain, power plants, raging rivers. This is how you can experience your morning shower.

Singing in the Rain

ARE YOU SINGING IN YOUR SHOWER? Are you acting like Gene Kelly in the film *Singin' in the Rain?* Water is irresistible—think about kids, sprinklers, and squirt guns. Why shouldn't your shower be playful? Try singing in the shower, or OM-ing in the shower. Imagine your shower as a new place everyday.

Reclaim yourself in your morning shower and set the stage for the day. By now you have gained awareness that the shower is a transformational experience. The next phase is choice. It is your time alone. It is the time in the day when you can fully choose your experience. The final part of the process is your intention. What is your intention for this shower? Is your intention to be invigorated? You may need healing. You may need peace of mind. You may need freedom: freedom from pain, freedom from sorrow, guilt, possessions, relationships, or responsibility. Your intention may be to shed whatever is holding you in bondage. So allow the power of the water to release you from it. Imagine it flowing down the drain.

Create new practices for your shower. Challenge yourself with shower rituals and create your own. There can be annual rituals for holidays throughout the year. For example, on Thanksgiving, focus on being grateful for every part of your body, your health, your family, your home, your intelligence, your gifts, and abilities. Tell every cell of your body that you are going to take on a life of gratefulness and gratitude. You can create rituals during different cycles of your life, at times of grieving, depression, illness, or joy.

The smallest changes you make in your daily shower can have astronomical effects. Historically there were few products offered for your shower. Zest deodorant soap promised to wake you up. Ivory's bar soap promise was purity. And Dove cleansing bar touted its cleansing-cream richness. Today there is a whole new array of products created for your shower. Every fragrance, every texture, every color, and every bottle configuration is available. Be adventuresome: These products are in almost every store. Wander the aisles and explore what resonates with you.

Smell is the most powerful of our five senses. Never underestimate the power that it has over your mental, physical, and spiritual states. Experiment with different smells according to your moods. On days that you feel lazy, tired or depressed use an invigorating citrus flavor like lemon or orange. On mornings you wake up anxious or fearful or nervous, you may want to choose lavender, chamomile, or clary sage. You way want to choose a sensual smell to feel sexy. There are many great books on the market about aromatherapy to help you choose a scent for your particular needs.

The temperature of your shower makes a world of difference in your experience. A tepid or cooler shower can wake you up and invigorate you. A very hot shower can bring comfort and ease into your day. Recently shower hardware has become available that has automatic presets for the temperature. This is a wonderful feature, but don't let it lock you into a habit. Make sure you vary your shower temperature.

Your morning shower may be the only opportunity during the day when you have total freedom to make every single decision. Make the most of it.

Looking in the Mirror

> "*Our bodies communicate to us clearly and specifically, if we are willing to listen to them.*"—SHAKTI GAWAIN

W **HAT APPEARS BEFORE YOU** as you stand naked in front of your bathroom mirror? There are a myriad of answers to this question because we all have such a diverse experience of our bodies. Our culture has conflicting views of the body. On one hand, society views our nakedness as deviant. Sometimes, even the innocence of a naked baby is morally questioned. On the other hand, you can hardly turn on a television or look at a popular magazine without seeing blatant nudity and hypersexuality. We can't help but wonder if this contributes to the epidemic problem of eating disorders and sexual confusion in our culture. We live in a Barbie-doll culture where the expectations for us are confusing and ambivalent.

The gloriousness, the sacredness about women is that each of us is different. We have the same anatomy, but different latitudes and longitudes. We have to quit judging each other and ourselves with unattainable and unreasonable expectations. Many of us live in a constant state of anxiety about the next great diet or diet pill, the next great exercise, or the next great diet guru. Did any of us really grow up wondering what size our mothers or grandmothers were? What mattered was the pure experience of the relationship. Who even noticed a size?

As you look into the mirror look with love and acceptance—not judgment—at your body as it is *now*. Don't dwell on what you looked like in the past: when you were in school; before you were married; before you had babies; or how you might look if you lost ten or fifteen pounds by bathing-suit season. Focus instead on how wonderful and miraculous your body is at this present moment.

Our Disembodiment

WESTERN RELIGIONS TEACH in Genesis that we are *Imago Dei*—created in the image of God. If this is the promise of religion, why is it so difficult for many of us to look at ourselves in the mirror? What have we been taught that brings pain, fear, anxiety, panic at the image of our own nakedness? Accepting our naked bodies may be one of our greatest personal journeys.

Unfortunately, Western cultures have divided the body and soul: a division not made by Eastern cultures. Don't you think it's time to reconnect your body and soul? Your soul experiences life through your body: the container, the vessel, the organism by which it functions.

Seeing Who's in the Mirror

STRIVE TO ACCEPT YOUR BODY and your form. There is a purpose and a reason for you to have the body you were born with. Our bodies are the stories of our lives. With each scar, each stretch mark, they record the events and the journeys we have experienced. Our bodies are holy recording devices. Be aware of the journey your body takes over time. Be mindful of this remarkable journey on which you embark daily with your body.

Let your body be your guide. Regular observation of your body is a health issue. If you regularly observe your body, you will notice inconsistencies: lumps, skin color changes, melanomas. While eight out of ten breast lumps are not cancerous, 70 percent of all breast cancers are found through breast self-exams. Keeping an eye on your body can literally save your life.

You may enjoy annointing your body daily with oil or cream. For many this may be uncomfortable to begin with, but over time you will look forward to reconnecting with your body everyday. Try choosing a scent according to your mood. Different aromas have distinct emotional and physiological effects. Your skin is an astounding organ. Your skin controls the temperature of your body and protects your body from bacteria and germs. Start with cream or oil at the top of your body and move down. Do so with great love, reverence, and respect for your body. It is a fragile, sacred instrument that we must nurture, respect, and care for. It is your body, after all, that enables you to experience all of life.

Breakfast

"All happiness depends on a leisurely breakfast."—JOHN GUNTHER

WHAT MEAL IS REGULARLY SKIPPED, overlooked, and underestimated? You guessed it. Breakfast is the most abused, disrespected, irreverent meal of the day. Breakfast is also the most fragmented meal of the day. People eat while running out the door, racing for the bus, and driving the car. The common breakfast scene for many of us is a toaster pastry in our pocket, coffee in one hand, briefcase and car keys in the other.

Breakfast has also turned into a junk-food fest: cereal bars, instant drinks, microwaveable packets of food. This is not to say that many of these things are not nutritious. But many of them are filled with excessive fat, sugar, and a tremendous number of calories. Complicating this is that most of this food is eaten standing, on the run, or in the car.

The worst offense is skipping breakfast. If you eat supper at 7:00 p.m., then skip breakfast the next morning, you are literally depriving your body of nourishment for 15 hours. Your body doesn't have what it needs to function and your metabolism is slowed down for the entire day.

Just because breakfast has "fast" in it doesn't mean it should be a race.

Breaking Fast

THE WORD "BREAKFAST" derives from the phrase "breaking the fast." We fast while we sleep. Breaking that fast should make breakfast the most joyful meal of the day. You have lived through the night and are beginning a new day. It is a new-ness and beginning that sets the stage—sets the table—for the day.

Do you remember the breakfasts at your grandmother's as a child? Do you remember the smells, the sounds that would wake you from your sleep? Do you remember the expecta-tion of what you might find when you walked into the kitchen? You knew that it would be something warm, something nu-tritious, something nourishing, something yummy. You knew that you were being comforted and loved.

Breakfast is also the first chance for the family to gather each day. As difficult as it may be, everyone needs to sit down and eat together. Even if it is only five minutes, that's five minutes together. Commit to five minutes, anything over that is grace. Remember: the faster you eat the more you eat. The longer you chew, the better your digestion. The slower you eat, the greater the production of saliva that facilitates the digestive process.

Creating breakfast is a mindfulness experience. You can buy inexpensive, bright-colored dishes or use playful napkins.

When you eat, it is important to eat mindfully and intentionally. Pause before you start eating and look at your food. Be thankful for your food, your day, your time with those you love. Consider the importance of being grateful for your food and ask a blessing over your food. Be thankful for the farmers that toiled for your food and the people who prepared it. This conveys gratitude and respect for the nourishment on your plate and the process that brought it there.

Are you too busy for breakfast? You are giving up a lot more than breakfast. According to an April 1999 study published by *The Journal of the American College of Nutrition*, people who eat breakfast consumed less fat and more carbohydrates, had a higher intake of essential vitamins and minerals, and lower serum cholesterol, which leads to a lower instance of heart disease.

Researchers from the Georgia Centenarian Study recently reported that people who reach the age of 100 tend to consume breakfast more regularly than those who skip the first meal of the day.

Dozens of studies show that people who eat plenty of fruits and vegetables generally have a lower risk of heart disease, cancer, and other chronic diseases.

Type 2 diabetes in children is rising to epidemic proportions. A healthy breakfast is the biggest disease prevention tool for children.

Medical studies have found a connection among eating breakfast, learning ability, attention span, and general well-being. They have also found a connection among skipping breakfast, weight gain, and memory impairment.

Eating breakfast increases the metabolic rate by 25 percent, which is one of the reasons why people report feeling better early in the morning.

The American Heart Association suggests that you may be more prone to diabetes and obesity if you skip breakfast because breakfast helps control your appetite for the rest of the day.

Break Feast

YOU DON'T HAVE TO TRY TO WORK in the time to cook a huge breakfast. It only takes 5–10 minutes to eat a bowl of cereal with low-fat milk and fruit. Try yogurt mixed with your cereal. If you don't like traditional breakfast food, eat a sandwich. Eat frozen waffles or pancakes with fruit or light syrup. This is a great time to be creative with what's in the refrigerator. Mix leftover vegetables from last night's dinner with scrambled eggs. What matters is that you are eating something and that you are eating something relatively healthy: preferably with a serving of fruit and some fiber. In eating breakfast, you have shown respect for your body, your family, and the importance of beginning your day in an intentional manner.

The Morning News

"Men are disturbed not by things that happen, but by their opinion of the things that happen."—EPICTETUS

ON TELEVISION TODAY, there is a regular morning show on almost every network channel with guests and co-hosts bringing you today's soft news. They are filled with human interest stories; what's new in the home; tidbits on relationships; cultural profiles; celebrity sightings; and breaking developments concerning your health and happiness. These morning shows have become a form of social conditioning: what is expected of you, what you should wear, what you should drive, what you should look like, what you should anticipate. These shows set a personal agenda that may or may not be in tune with your spirit.

Infotainment

OUR GOOD MORNING SHOWS feature what is called "infotainment." It is a fusing of information and entertainment that our American culture has become addicted to. Our lives have become woven together by sound bites and video clips. We expect weather every fifteen minutes, traffic on the half hour, and the cult of celebrity in between. We expect an entertainment aspect to everything in our lives. The media is sending all of this to us. But we have a choice—a filtering process of what we take into our lives. We are being overloaded with too much mindless information and we have to decide what is personally useful.

Continuing Education

CHOOSE WHAT YOU WANT to actively learn in the morning. What aspects of our popular culture do you really need to know? Instead of the morning news being background noise, intentionally screen for information that matters to you. You can select the information that will feed your spirit and benefit your life. Look to the morning as a time to get information about what is going on in the world—not news-wise—but rather information on books or medical studies. Choose to listen to the information that has to do with enriching your life. Actively structure your watching or listening for things you are interested in. Try alternative media sources like NPR or the BBC for different perspectives. Use the morning news as a classroom. Take the snippets of information you are receiving, find something that interests you, then use that as a starting point on a journey to other sources of information: libraries, Internet searches, bookstores, etc.

Commuting

"If you do what you've always done, you'll get what you've always gotten."—ANONYMOUS

MILLIONS OF PEOPLE EVERYDAY spend countless hours in their automobiles. According to the 2000 Census, 34 percent of Americans spend 30 minutes or more each way on their commute. That's over 250 hours a year just getting back and forth to work. It has become a competition of me against the other for the best seat on the train, the fastest lane on the highway, the last spot on the bus. Increasingly, we are mad and frustrated at others for being in our way. Worse, we begin to feel we are victimized in this space—out of control and insignificant. These kinds of psychological dynamics lead to horrible consequences resulting in violence and road rage. We know that road rage is on the rise. People can't take being trapped in their cars, stuck in traffic, or late.

Planes, Trains, and Automobiles

COMMUTING HAS BECOME a time of alienation and aggression. Several recently-released scientific studies suggest the more hassled drivers feel by their morning commute, the more verbally abusive they are to co-workers. These drivers also attempt to sabotage productive efforts at work. Maybe it's time for us to gain a new perspective on our commute. Two ways you can do this: change what you are doing or change your attitude about what you are doing. Either eliminate your commute or alter your outlook about your commute. We can't rely upon Detroit or Tokyo because the auto industry has given us options and add-ons like videos, phones, and GPS that lead us away from ourselves to an even more distracted state. The goal of the Metropolitan Transportation Authority is efficiency, not your spiritual or mental health. You have the power to make the choice for the everyday activity of commuting to be a spiritual experience.

Transformational Space

COMMUTING IS PACKED with options for your spiritual growth. Your commute has the potential of becoming a classroom, a chapel, a behaviorist laboratory, a choir loft. For many of us, commuting is, in fact, a rare time when we are alone. You can use this time to learn something new. Books-on-tape transform your commute into a classroom experience. Used

as a time for prayer—perhaps with prayer beads or music—
your commute becomes a reflective moment in a chapel.

It can become a behaviorist laboratory. Pick an attitude
that you want to change like anger or pessimism. Then find
and listen to tapes on that subject as an opportunity to grow
psychologically and emotionally.

Your commute can be a experience in a choir loft. If you
love music and you love singing, it is a time for you to join
in song: an activity that is emotionally, psychologically, and
spiritually beneficial. Psychologist Dr. David Wiesenthal of
York University in Toronto found in his studies on commuting that, "Deep breathing exercises help shed tension as does
listening to one's favorite kind of music." What a wonderful
way to start your day. Redesign the space within your car with
comforting objects, a flower, a shawl, prayer beads.

Last but not least, commuting can be a time of spiritual
transformation. You don't have to think of this time as wasted,
lost, or not meaningful. This is a time to experience yourself as part of the human family. You are not up and against
the driver in the car beside you. We are all sharing the highway. We are all on merging paths. We must give and take
and share on our commute. Realize that we are all together.
It is an illusion that we are all separate competing for the same
resource. We are sharing it. Even being alone, we are together
as we commute.

Practice virtues on your commute. Take steps in a public display of spirituality. Allow someone to merge in front
of you. When someone unintentionally cuts you off, smile
and bless them in their preoccupation. Pray they may become
more aware. When it begins to storm, pray for all drivers on

the road, for everyone's safety. It is your choice. As you commute, you may choose to create anxiety, anger, frustration and alienation, or you may choose to create a time for self-reflection, mindfulness and personal growth.

The
Power of
Surrender

S I PUSHED OPEN the old log cabin door, two black scorpions rushed across the planked floors and disappeared into the fireplace. An unfriendly welcome, but I knew there was no turning back. A faint light filtered through closed shutters. It smelled musty and moldy, I was sure the room hadn't been opened in years. The old wood floor creaked as I slowly walked across to open the shutters to invite the daylight in. I was standing in the midst of dancing cobwebs and swirling dust. I had begun a journey with no map, no directions and no clear destination.

In the stark silence of that moment, a certain sense of peace swept across the room and engulfed me. I knew that this moment would change the rest of my life.

The cabin had no electricity, no water, no gas, no kitchen, and no bathroom. I surveyed the outside and found the outhouse and a rain barrel on the far side of the cabin. Back on the front porch, I snuggled into an old rocker that had been left behind. And in anticipation of the days ahead, I pulled a tissue from my pocket to write on.

As I began making a list of "how-to" books I would need on plumbing, construction, electrical work, a rush of power washed deeply through my body. I grinned as I rocked. In this primitive cabin in the north Georgia mountains, I was a long way from my previous life at the World Trade Center.

I WAS WORKING IN NEW YORK CITY, flying back and forth to Atlanta each week. My life was a race. But I had all the trappings of success measured by our culture. I was set on a model of doing everything faster and better than any of my competitors. I was a stock broker at a large securities firm. My aspiration was to have it all. I am the oldest daughter in a family of seven children and groomed for self-reliance. From the time I was a little girl I wanted to be a successful woman. For me, that meant having an upwardly mobile career, husband, children, a nice home, a great car, elegant clothes, and fabulous vacations. I constantly worked to keep a perfect dress size and drove the ultimate driving machine to match.

My life was very well calculated and moving at a planned, orchestrated pace, when one day—in a split second—everything stopped. I had landed at the airport as usual early Monday morning and grabbed a cab to the World Trade Center. I got out of the cab, entered the building, and headed for the elevator. All of a sudden, my chest was so tight I could hardly breathe. We were all packed into the elevator as usual, but this time as it sped up to my office, I thought I was having a heart attack.

I lurched off the elevator and lay against the wall. Three hours later, I was still against the same wall and hadn't moved an inch. An attentive security guard had noticed—and perhaps because he had seen it before—made a diagnosis of a panic attack. Little did I know that would be first of many to follow. It wasn't too long until insomnia began to accompany the panic attacks. I became obsessively aware of the people that surrounded me each day.

I felt that we looked and acted like zombies, people trained to do the same thing over and over again. I noticed how people were buying lunch from a sidewalk cart then mindlessly eating as they walked away. Everywhere I looked, everyone and everything began to look the same. We were all in a trance. My well-designed life had started to unravel.

Later, still in New York, I was studying for my commodity boards, when I stumbled upon an old Thoreau journal in the apartment where I was staying. Little did I know his words would change my life forever:

"I went to the woods because I wished to live deliberately, to front only the essential facts of life, and see if I could not learn what it had to teach, and not, when I came to die, discover that I had not lived."

My response to that famous passage was shock, confusion, and indescribably immense sadness. Was I living an intentional life? How in the heck did I know what the essential facts of life were? Have I really lived at all? Is living in the middle of a rat race really living?

I had not been in the woods since I was a child. I knew nothing about nature and the mere thought that it held the possibility of teaching me something both intrigued and terrified me. A fundamental shift occurred in that moment and I knew there was no turning back.

Two days later, I quit my job. One week later, I purchased a farm with an old log cabin that sat by a lake. There wasn't even a road into the cabin from a main road. I had to hike to the cabin for the first year. I was determined to live up to Thoreau's challenge. I was going to face the challenge of living an intentional life. I would release the life that I had so masterfully orchestrated and designed. I would turn this land into a working farm. My surrender had begun.

IT WASN'T UNTIL SOME YEARS LATER that I would really understand the spiritual practice of surrender. Growing up in a competitive sports and business-driven family, surrender was a dirty word. Surrender meant loser, failure, being conquered. The image of the white flag with the defeated person marching across the battle field accompanies the word surrender. Surrender was—and still is—the most difficult spiritual practice to embrace.

There is an old saying I love that says, "There is my plan, and then there is God's plan, and my plan doesn't count." Surrender is releasing your ego and your attachment to life the way you have constructed it. When one embraces surrender, it is an act of trust. In surrender, you are trusting and joining a power that is greater than your own. When you practice surrender, there is synergy in every action of your life. Life becomes exciting, dynamic, and meaningful. You know that you are living an intentional life because you are fully present and completely yourself in every situation. You live in a state of confidence.

After I left the brokerage firm and moved to the woods, I had the privilege to study with many great spiritual teachers who each lived holy lives of surrender on a daily basis. One of my great teachers was former U.S. President and Nobel Peace Prize winner Jimmy Carter. President Carter taught a class in ethics when I was in seminary at Emory University. He talked about his experience in the White House and the difficult decisions he had to make. He knew his choices were not what many of the politicians in Washington wanted. Very often these decisions were not popular. President Carter understood that he would not get re-elected if he made certain decisions. Yet he surrendered to truth rather than political expediency. He would not compromise who he was.

After he lost his bid for reelection, President Carter was somewhat depressed and confused. He made a conscious decision to surrender to the pain of his loss and to devote his life to making the world a better place for others.

In class, he told us about traveling to monitor elections in dangerous third-world countries, because he believed that every person, no matter what their position in life, had a right to the ballot box.

When his wife, Rosalynn and he traveled to Africa, they discovered that a tremendous number of people there were infected with a horrible living worm that grows in the body. This disgusting worm is contracted from the water in Africa. This worm grows in the bodies of people and gets to be quite large. It can cause horrible pain and death. President Carter and Rosalynn were overwhelmed with compassion for the suffering of these people. They made it their goal to eradicate this terrible condition. They are a living example of the spiritual practice of surrender. They embrace a life open to each new circumstance on their path as an opportunity to surrender, learn and become someone new.

NOT SO LONG AGO, I was sitting in the corner of the stall at my stables after foaling out a mare, and I reflected on the odyssey of my spiritual path. I now live in the woods full-time and it has taught me much. Many lessons have come to me as I built this farm and transformed my life. Many holy people have inspired me along the way: the ninety-year-old farmer down the road that still makes hominy and cans his own sauerkraut; the eighty-eight-year-old, near-blind woman who made me a prize-winning quilt; my elderly patient who has survived every malady imaginable, but shows up to group each week with a smile on her face. There are so many simple, holy people in the woods who can teach you a lot, if you just slow down and listen. There are also the four-legged angels that inspire me daily: my dogs, cats, and horses.

Most people would see the surrender of Wall Street to a log cabin in the North Georgia woods as opposite ends of the scale. By comparison to what others have done, I realize every day that on my spiritual journey I still have very far to go.

It takes one courageous step at a time. People who live extraordinary lives are in fact ordinary people who make choices that lead to extraordinary circumstances. These choices are often very small, and these choices are available to you.

Working

"Work is love made visible. And if you cannot work with love but only with distaste, it is better that you should leave your work and sit at the gate of the temple and take alms of those who work with joy."—KAHLIL GIBRAN

WHEN WE MENTION WORK, the image that comes to mind for most in the Western world is one of productivity, time and motion studies, assembly lines, and cubicles. The American workplace is possibly the most spiritually-barren space many of us ever inhabit. The requirement to make business decisions based on bottom-line thinking, by definition, almost always eliminates making decisions based on spiritual merit. Maintaining a spiritual orientation in the American earnings-per-share workplace is an extraordinary challenge. The paths of profit and enlightenment almost never cross.

A great number of employees in the industrial world are dissatisfied with their life at work. Today, work is experienced almost exclusively as an avenue to make money, an avenue to purchase consumer goods. Work is largely experienced as addiction: workaholism; escapism from one's self and one's family; our primary expression of identity. For many, work is experienced as nothing more than apathetic habituation. It is hollow, empty, and meaningless. Work is a mundane task that earns us a benefit package. Our Western culture has stripped work of its meaning and consequently of the dignity of performing it. Is it possible for us to view labor as dignified, the laborers as noble?

Inner and Outer Work

THE INTENTION IS FOR US to experience work as a call of life, a vocation, as a community; to understand work as a healthy balance among mind, body, and soul. Ancient spiritual liturgy teaches us that work is holy; that work is a privilege. Freud said work is the basis of sanity. Work should be the source of our dignity.

In the Benedictine monastic order of the Christian church, work is holy because it makes us "whole-ly." Work is participation in creation. Not a punishment or a penance. Work is purposeful and valuable. According to all spiritual traditions, it is our job on this earth to continue the work of creation. Work is experienced as interconnectedness of all creation.

Most contemporary work, however, is divorced from the nobility of engaging in the process of co-creating the earth. By co-creation, we mean that each of us is participating in the divine process of creation. Writing, teaching, business, whatever it is you do is co-creation with the Divine. We literally become the physical tools: the hands, the feet, the voice, of the Creator so that we can facilitate the promise of the world becoming a better place.

Work should mean prosperity and spiritual growth. We can grow spiritually at work. We were created to experience work as life-giving; work as a spiritual journey; work as co-creation; work as abundance. Begin experiencing your work as participating in something larger than yourself. Your exterior work should reflect your interior work.

Spiritual Classrooms

THERE IS A SPIRITUAL SOLUTION to the problem of perception of work today. The solution is to change your perception of your job by experiencing it as a spiritual classroom, somewhere where you can learn and grow. Understand that everyone at work is there for a reason. Each person you encounter has the possibility to challenge and ultimately transform you. You have choices about how you approach and handle situations. You learn a great deal about others from work and there are lessons you can learn about yourself as well. It is spirituality that enables us to recognize events in this larger, universal context. One of the most common business problems, for example, is dealing with anger that arises from office politics and perceived unfairness. Addressing situations in a mindful way can help to circumvent this problem.

Your attitude is a choice. You may choose to change your approach to work. This is an invitation for you to experience work as a spiritual path. This job is a classroom, and when you stop learning, go to another classroom. Try to approach your work with curiosity. Do your best to be grateful for the ability to work. Practice listening skills. Make an effort to be respectful of your co-workers. Look at their diversity as an opportunity to learn. Consider looking for the greater good in the smallest task.

How do you do this? Work is about mindfulness and awareness. Make an effort to treat all those around you with dignity. Your co-workers are as much a part of creation as you are. Re-imagine yourself at work. Recreate your personal space at work. Pack your lunch differently. Try changing your dress. Examine your conversations with co-workers. Put them to the test of ancient Sufi wisdom: is it true, is it necessary, is it fair?

Try to remember that conflict is an excellent circumstance for growth. You don't have to react immediately, rather reflect first. Reconnect with your spirituality before you respond to a situation. Breathe. Center yourself. Carefully consider your response.

When we explore and revise who we are with respect to our work and our co-workers, we discover our true passion—we uncover who we were created to be and what we were created to do.

Walking

"He who sits still in a house all the time may be the greatest vagrant of all; but the saunterer, in the good sense, is no more vagrant than the meandering river, which is all the while sedulously seeking the shortest course to the sea. For every walk is a sort of crusade."—
HENRY DAVID THOREAU

---

*T*HERE IS NO PERSON KNOWN and revered for walking more than Henry David Thoreau. For Thoreau, walking was a spiritual practice, an opportunity to explore nature, an activity that led to him becoming one of the foremost conservationists of all time. Thoreau warned us that when we do not experience nature in its fullest, we may eventually erode our freedom and wildness which is our lifeline to creation and the Creator.

Thoreau challenged us to perceive the concept of walking as a crusade or an adventure with intention.

Challenge yourself, recapture the original concept of sauntering as discussed in Thoreau's essay "Walking." You may develop the passion he had for its utter simplicity.

Taking Spiritual Steps

SAUNTER, SAUNTER, SAUNTER: it is an historical practice. Buddha walked from village to village and taught with disciples for most of his life. Jesus went from town to town on foot. Mahatma Gandhi's 150-mile-long Salt March was his reaction to the British occupation of India's salt mines. He didn't stop walking after that. Rather, he lived on his feet, walking for social justice and transforming a nation. Dr. Martin Luther King, Jr. walked the roads of Mississippi, Alabama, and Georgia, seeking an end to the hatred that separated a country. Susan B. Anthony spent her entire life walking so that women could participate in the democratic process through voting. Walking—as an empowering, community building force—is a recurring theme of social justice.

Reverence for the spiritual path of walking has been lost to the convenience of moving sidewalks, escalators, elevators, treadmills, Stairmasters, and of course, cars. Why limit your walking to physical exercise? Begin to experience walking as an opportunity for spiritual exercise. Most religious and spiritual paths, Monastics, Islamic Sufis, Buddhists, partake in the spiritual practice of walking meditations.

Vietnamese Buddhist monk, Thich Nhat Hanh, famous for his writings and instruction on walking meditation, teaches that the intention of your walk is to be present in the moment. The essence of the walk is two fold: It is about mindfulness and awareness. Mindfulness is being fully present in the moment. As we begin to think about the anxieties and fears of the past or the future, we can release them when walking and return fully to the present moment. As you walk, experience the fullness of your soul, your body, and your mind as you are moving. There is a grounded rhythm and flow that can be experienced as a symphony. In the practice of awareness, we are aware of our experience in the wind, the temperature, the sun, the season, the birds, the alchemy of Nature. All of our senses become keenly aware and profoundly energetic. In the dance of mindfulness and awareness, we empty ourselves into the moment as our senses are heightened.

Pilgrimages are still a part of almost every spiritual tradition and belief system. From historical times until today, Jews go to Jerusalem; Christians go to the Holy Land; Muslims go to Mecca. In the process of a pilgrimage, you are participating in a community. And whether rich or poor, ignorant or educated, we are all journeying the same path toward the same destination. A pilgrimage becomes a metaphor for our spiritual journey through this life. When you reach the destination of your pilgrimage, you experience renewal and wholeness.

Walking 101

GET OUT OF YOUR CAR, get off your bike, get off the bus one stop early, and walk. Use this time for reflection and awareness. Notice the birds, the sky, the people around you. See, smell, listen. Follow in the footsteps taken in the noble historical practice of walking. Better still, don't just walk. Challenge the curiosity of the discoverer that lies within you. Take the less traveled road, change your route, choose a different path. Remember the advice of Thoreau: "We should go forth on the shortest walk, perchance, in the spirit of undying adventure, never to return."

Exercise

"Do your thing and you will have the power."—RALPH WALDO EMERSON

I **T IS CRITICAL**—literally for the length and quality of our lives—that we educate ourselves about exercise and the importance of exercise. It is essential in all the stages of our life. Exercise keeps us fit. It prevents heart disease, cancer, arthritis, and a host of other medical conditions. It lowers blood pressure, lowers cholesterol, and controls blood sugar. A lack of physical activity has tremendous effects on us psychologically. Robert M. Butler, MD of Mt. Sinai Medical School in New York said, "If exercise could be packaged into a pill it would be the single most prescribed and beneficial medication in the nation."

The Cleveland Clinic has found that exercise has been proven to reduce stress, anxiety, and depression. They have found exercise strengthens and builds muscle tone and bones; increases energy levels; reduces body fat; and helps increase the strength of the heart. They have also found that exercise is an effective treatment for depression.

We now have evidence from many studies that show exercise stimulates the immune system. Exercise stimulates "natural killer cells" which play a vital role in fighting cancer cells, bacteria, and viruses.

Expand Your Concept of Exercise

EXERCISE IN AMERICA has been experienced as punishment and narrowly associated with health clubs and weight loss. Exercise is the essential, pivotal element of the mind- body-soul balance because it literally affects all three. When we exercise, we display reverence for the magnificence of our bodies. If you think your body is holy, you need to be exercising. If we are indeed made in the image of God as sacred scriptures tell us, then we need to align ourselves with our spiritual energies. Your balance requires some form of movement of your body.

Just as historical Eastern practices like yoga, tai chi, or chi gong are readily understood as spiritual forms of exercise, we can apply the same principle to any form of exercise by viewing it as increasing the alignment of our body and soul. Even jumping jacks, lifting weights, or your elliptical machine can be experienced as spiritual exercise.

Find Your Rhythm

FIND THE EXERCISE that fits the rhythm of your body and brings you balance. If you try something and you aren't en-

joying it—if you just can't keep doing it after a month or so—
try something else. You will find something that clicks for
you and you'll know it. Walking, kickboxing, yoga, dance.
Move your body and you will find the rhythm of your soul.

Shopping

"Yesterday is a cancelled check; tomorrow is a promissory note; today is the only cash you have—so spend it wisely."—KAY LYONS

SHOPPING IS A DIFFERENT EXPERIENCE for each of us. It can be a leisure activity. It can take your mind off the anxiety or stress of a situation or event. Shopping can lead you out of isolation and loneliness into a sense of community. It can be ritualized as a holiday experience, or simply a time to purchase something. Shopping can provide different experiences for our lives. You may want time alone. You may feel the urge to call an old friend you haven't seen in a long time and reconnect as you saunter through the mall. You may not be in the mood for the holidays. But going shopping and experiencing the music and the decorations may be the inspiration you need. You may be wearing an old a sweater given to you by someone in a past relationship. And shopping for a new one may be the key to your letting go. Shopping is an avenue to many possibilities.

Fill the Hole

THERE CAN ALSO BE A DARK SIDE to shopping today. Some people shop in an attempt to fill an empty space in their lives. For many people, shopping can be an addiction. They experience shopping as exhilarating, fun, addictive, or better than sex. They do it during the day, at night, in catalogs, in stores, on the Internet. Shopping may become an escape—a distraction, like gambling. To seek a certain product on sale becomes an obsessive quest—a search for the Holy Grail at 40 percent off. It becomes an addiction, because it must be done over and over again as the rewards are fleeting. Shopping can be experienced as the pure pleasure of accumulation. We can be led to believe the commercial lie that ownership becomes the key to satisfaction and happiness. The more you own, the happier you will be. The fact is, this is simply not true.

Can we say that for some people in our culture today, shopping has become a religion? Assess the time you are spending shopping. Are you shopping to fill a void? As it feeds your closet, is it feeding your soul?

Don't Shop 'Til You Drop

WE ARE NOT PROPOSING that people should stop shopping. But when you purchase something, it should at least be meaningful. Whether you purchase a sweater, a scarf, or a pair of shoes, create the experience that purchasing this object is meaningful. In taking your hard-earned money and buying goods, you should feel altered, different, and new.

You may want to buy things that remind you of your childhood, or make you feel safe—purchases that make you feel significant, expressive. Your buys are an expression of who you are. Your purchase can have more meaning than to be just fashionable, stylish, cool, or have a popular designer label.

You may want to develop a new attitude about shopping. See it as an observation of the expression of diverse cultures. Experience shopping as an exploration of handicraft, artistic expression, cultural bias, an interpretation of utilitarianism. Consider the store as a museum where shopping is a process of observation and exploration of art. Look at colors, style, fabrics, and design. Marvel in the creativity of these products. Your challenge could be not "shop 'til you drop," but to experience shopping as playground of possibilities.

Listening

"With the gift of listening comes the gift of healing."— CATHERINE DE HUECK

*I*N THE WEST, listening is not recognized as a skill that takes training to develop. To so many of us, silence denotes ignorance. In truth, silence—in the form of listening—is a fine art. Though today's hectic world leaves us little time for reflection and listening, it is a skill any of us can and should attempt to master.

When we think of listening, we think of it as part of communication. There are two primary actions that take place in our communications model: talking and listening. In the world today, the primary focus of the communication process is talking. In truth, listening is perhaps the more important component in the communication model.

Americans have a fascination with talk shows. Most of these shows are filled with people talking faster and louder than each other. And when you think about it, nobody is listening. We have turned into a culture where faster, louder, and staccato talking has overshadowed the grace and dignity of the humble and sacred practice of listening.

Hearing vs. Listening

LISTENING IS ACTUALLY TAUGHT, but seldom in mainstream culture. It should be though. Because if we were taught listening, the world would be a totally different place. Most of us assume that hearing and listening are the same experience. But in fact, they are very different. Hearing is a passive act. Hearing is stimulation of auditory nerves in the ear by sound waves. It is one of our five basic senses, an evolutionary defense mechanism. Listening is active: a practice learned through conscious effort. Because it is perceived as passive, listening is not valued in our culture. In truth, listening is a very dynamic, engaging spiritual practice.

Listening demands the full presence of the listener. We live in a world of distracted people with their minds racing as they drive, work, and walk the streets of the city. Listening requires that you be present in the here and now. As we listen, we become a midwife, helping something to be born in the person talking. In the pure act and presence of listening, we give life to the experiences and words of others.

The Art of Listening

LISTENING IS A SACRED ACT of reverence. The skilled listener is able to listen without judgment, with an openness that expresses acceptance, vulnerability, and presence.

When we experience listening as a gift, it becomes the ultimate act of hospitality. In the act of hospitality we treat all persons as guests—special and invited into your personal inner sanctum. Throughout all religions, welcoming the stranger is one of the most time honored spiritual practices.

Listening becomes your own spiritual teacher. Listening teaches you the virtues of patience, silence, and awareness. Listening requires you to be fully present in the moment and therefore your life becomes more meaningful. Finally, listening is the ultimate experience of relationship, where you enter into the act of communion and truly become greater than yourself.

How many times a day can you make the ordinary practice of listening a spiritually rewarding experience?

Reading

"You must understand the whole of life not just one little part of it. That is why you must read, that is why you must look at the skies, that is why you must sing, and dance, and write poems, and suffer, and understand, for all that is life." —KRISHNAMURTI

---

*W*E ARE CURRENTLY EXPERIENCING a resurgence of reading in our culture. Oprah Winfrey opened the door with her book club. And the morning shows followed by making recommendations for the hot new titles. Bookstores are the latest hang-out.

It is assumed that all methods of reading are identical—that reading is reading. But in fact, nothing could be further from the truth. In our culture, we have been trained to read critically. When we critically read, we read for information, entertainment, details. We engage in dialog with the author. We question and interact with the information we are reading. We are actively engaged cognitively. Critical reading includes everything from the daily newspaper to summer novels.

Another approach to reading is called formative reading. Formative reading is "reading for the soul." It is dwelling reverently on a text and its meaning. Formative reading is experiential: It opens the reader to personal and communal transformation. It is not what is said in the text, but rather how the text can be absorbed so that it has personal meaning.

Surrender

OUR SOULS ARE TIRED and need nourishment. We are overstimulated in this fast paced world. We feel drained and exhausted. Formative reading creates wonderful awareness and profound reflection. Formative reading creates new depth in our lives. We can live in the world with new perspectives. Formative reading is an ancient spiritual path that can offer benefits to our culture as we relearn this ancient spiritual practice.

Historically, we have formatively read in all major religions and spiritualities. Sacred scriptures are an example of this: the Bible in Christianity, the Torah in Judaism, Islam's Koran, the Upanishads and the Vedas in Hinduism, the Discourses of Buddha in Buddhism, the I Ching in Taoism, and the teachings of the mystics through out the ages.

We can also formatively read the great spiritual thinkers throughout human history: Thomas Merton, Henri Nowen, Teresa Avila, Anthony De Mello, Rumi, Julian of Norwich, plus other spiritual and inspiring authors.

Formative reading has two elements: trust and surrender. You must trust the author and the text. Surrender to the text. You do not argue or talk with the text, rather you surrender to the power of the words. You immerse yourself in the text. It is as if the words are droplets of rain softly falling over your soul. You become formed by the message of the author.

Words, Words, Words

ONE WAY TO ALLOW WORDS to surround you and envelop you is to read the same words over and over again. When you read the same passage at different times in your life, you re-experience the words. The text will mean something different each time you read it. You will likely have many different revelations on the same text at different times and in different situations.

Another technique is to read a text once, then contemplate the message in silence for a time.

Formative reading feeds the soul. Soak in the words. Allow them to drench you. Let them permeate your whole body, lingering with you long after you have moved on from your reading. You have the ability to be greatly transformed by the spiritual writers of the past and the present.

CHAPTER THREE

The
Practice

I **WOKE UP IN THE DARK,** startled by the sound of the telephone. I was confused and somewhat disoriented. I couldn't remember how long I had been lying there. I didn't even make an attempt to answer the telephone as it continued to ring. The fact is it had been ringing for weeks. I hadn't been answering it and every time I heard the ring I shuddered inside.

My daughter opened my bedroom door and sat on the bed. She kissed me gently on the cheek and smiled. "Mom, you are going to have to get up," she said. "You have to eat something. You have to talk. Please, you are scaring me."

Just then, the phone rang again. Before I could stop her my daughter reached for the phone and said, "Hello…yes, she is here, Mr. Landers. But she won't speak to anyone. She won't eat. She won't get out of bed." There was a silence and she said, "Mom, it's John Landers. And he said if you don't talk to him on this phone right now he is coming out here and dragging you out of that bed."

"I will not move. Tell him to go away."

My daughter, still on the phone, said to me, "Mom, Mr. Landers will give you 30 seconds to get on this phone or he is on his way."

I was panicked. I just wanted to move to another state. I wanted to disappear. I never wanted to be seen in public again. Not after what I had done. But I knew John, and if I didn't talk to him, I knew he really would come out and get me. Reluctantly, I took the call, a call that would give me the encouragement to leave my shame and begin again.

TEN MONTHS BEFORE, I was facilitating my regular cardiac wellness class at the local hospital, listening to my geriatric patients lament the enormous cost of prescription drugs. Some of them could hardly afford to eat and pay rent. This was a continual conversation at our group. The general public really doesn't appreciate how stressful it is for our older people to struggle with their day-to-day finances just to live. I listened to their struggles for years. And one day one of them said, "Dr. Hall, why don't you run for office and help us? You understand what we go through. We would all help you if you would run for the legislature." The rest of the group chimed in and encouraged me to run for office. I shrugged the offer off, but on into the night the idea gnawed at me.

I knew nothing about politics. I had never run for any office in my life. I had worked with the disadvantaged, the poor, the sick, and the disabled. But I was never a politician. I had seen firsthand the powerlessness in poverty and aging. I surely had a handle on what many people needed and what was missing in their lives, but I never considered throwing my hat into the political arena. It was a bizarre thought to me, but before I knew it, my cardiac group was out building support for my candidacy. People called and asked me make it official.

I began to analyze the situation. I had just earned my doctorate. I was educated, passionate, had an inordinate amount of energy, and loved people. Maybe I could run for office. But then the dark inner personal voices started clamoring. What if I lose? How embarrassing to lose in front of 30,000 people? How will I feel if they reject me? I am in the North Georgia mountains, and I am a progressive woman running in a rural area. Do I really have a chance?

It was the night before official Notice of Candidacy was due at the capitol in Atlanta. I was in knots trying to decide what to do. I sat on my back porch, overlooking the pasture as the sun was setting. I imagined that I was eighty years old, sitting in that same rocking chair, my granddaughter walked up to me and asked, "Grandma, what was the best thing you ever did in your life." I smiled at her and I answered, "Honey, the greatest thing I ever did was when a group of citizens asked me to run for office to represent them at the capitol. I was afraid that I would lose and be embarrassed. But Susie, I ran for that office. I risked everything and ran. That was the greatest thing I ever did."

Then I imagined that I was eighty years old, sitting in that same rocking chair, my granddaughter walked up to me, and asked, "Grandma, what was the worst thing you ever did in your life?" I had a disturbed look on my face and I answered, "Honey, the worst thing I ever did was when I was younger, a group of citizens asked me to run for office to represent them at the capitol. I was afraid that I would lose and I would be embarrassed. I did not run for office because I was afraid. I always will wonder if I would have won or not, and I wonder how it would have changed my life."

I woke up the next morning, drove to Atlanta, and registered to run for the Georgia legislature.

It was an amazing experience. My loving, loyal cardiac, pulmonary, and cancer patients were my volunteers for the election. It was such a blessing to see my campaign headquarters loaded with devoted workers. Some campaigned pulling their oxygen tanks behind them, some were in wheelchairs, some walked in walkers. They worked all day and night stuffing, stamping, answering telephones, campaigning around the community in our bright red shirts that read, "Kathleen Hall 2000."

I remember two sobering events that occurred right after the campaign had begun. My opponent approached me before a debate, shook my hand, and said, "Don't take what I say and do personally." I stared at him—shocked—and tried to decide how ominous his warning was. A week later, a seasoned politician sitting beside me at a fund raiser whispered in my ear, "Now that you are running for political office, you will really learn what hate is." I will never forget the chill that went up my spine.

Well, I lost the election. But I walked through many great fears along the trail. I learned one of the most valuable lessons in my life that year: that even by running and losing, you can win. I experienced what real community is: giving, sharing, loyalty, laughter, crying, and utter commitment to each other. I now know thousands of people that I never would have known. Every time I go to Wal-Mart today, there are many people that still shake my hand and tell me they voted for me, or that they spent hours putting signs up for me, or spent a night making cookies for a fundraiser. Running for political office was a profound spiritual experience and a lesson in humility. A public loss is a wonderful lesson in humility—and love.

I entered this political experience mindful of the spiritual practice of surrender. I promised to do every thing in my power to win the election, and to surrender to the painful lessons that I would learn in the process. I believe that the most valuable and profound lessons in spirituality are learned through suffering. We all suffer on some level many times in our life. The ultimate spiritual practice is how we choose to experience suffering and our response to suffering.

Remember that phone call I took from John Landers back when the wounds were still deep? When I took to my bed and I would not get out? I was so depressed and ashamed that I would not talk to anyone or leave my house. That day, John told me to come to our Rotary meeting, or he would drag me to it. I told him I was too embarrassed to show my face in public. John told me he would be proud to walk into Rotary with me. Proud that I ran an ethical, honest race. He assured me that getting 40 percent of the vote was respectable against a long-entrenched incumbent. One friend, of many, who stood by me through my recovery.

YEARS BEFORE MY ATTEMPT to become a state representative, I walked into my class at Emory with great anticipation because Nobel Peace Prize winner Bishop Desmond Tutu was my teacher. I expected him to be a large, tall, and strong man. I expected him to walk in a very deliberate, powerful manner and talk in an articulated slow cadence. He was supposed to be bigger than life. I had read everything I could about this man. For me he was literally a Christ-like figure to be awed and revered.

That day in class a tiny man stood before us. How could this little man—with an infectious laugh that could melt your heart—have changed the world? I would learn that it was his smile, his voice, and his boundless love for humankind.

That voice—passionate, heartbreaking, pleading, soft, loving, tender, holy. That angelic face. He has a look that can make you cry, scream, or want to swim the Atlantic Ocean to help him.

It has been one of the greatest privileges in my life to have personally experienced the holiness of this man. I can still hear his laughter echoing in my soul.

Bishop Tutu's life is the essence of spiritual practice. He has witnessed slaughter, hate, and truly the most violent acts of human beings. But never once has he responded with hatred, revenge, or retribution. To the murderer, the perpetrator, the racist, the hatemonger, it makes no difference. Bishop Tutu only sees the glowing face of Christ in all people and senses the presence of Christ in all experiences.

One morning, a student in our class asked him how he could not despise the whites in South Africa. What spiritual practice did he engage to deal with all the hate and violence? Bishop Tutu answered, "My practice is to see Christ in all people. I do not see color, not black, not white, just Christ."

He told this story:

"I was fast asleep in my home early one morning and was awoken by banging on my door. At my door was a young boy from a local school. He had awakened me to tell me that the boys at the school were going to march to the sea at sunrise. This was a huge problem because the white army did not permit the blacks to go to the beach. These young boys were determined to confront the injustice of such laws and had organized a march to the sea that morning. The boy who woke me was afraid and thought that the others might listen to me and it would save their lives. I knew I had to get to the boys imme-

diately so off I ran to the school. When I arrived
they were already lined up and ready to march.
They knew that the army knew about this march
and was waiting for them. I begged them to go
back to their homes and stop the march. The
young boys said they would not be stopped by
anyone and they were marching to the sea. I
knew that my only hope of stopping the
violence was to accompany the boys on the
march and be their spokesperson. So arm in arm
we departed. As we reached the sea, we saw the
army lined up in formation to keep the young
boys from advancing."

"As we marched, a young Lieutenant
approached us and said, 'Bishop Tutu, you must
turn these boys back to the village. You know
they are not allowed to go to the beach.' I
pleaded with the Lieutenant, as I watched the
other soldiers with their loaded rifles waiting for
orders. The Lieutenant was becoming
increasingly nervous and pleaded with me one
last time, 'Bishop, I will have to give the order
to open fire on the boys if they march on to the
sea.'"

"I looked into the beautiful blue eyes of the
Lieutenant, put his head in my hands and
explained that I knew he had orders and must do
what he must do. I said that I would lead the
boys to the ocean, therefore shoot me first. And
when you shoot me, I told the Lieutenant, know

that I love you, and that I forgive you. Then I kissed him on the cheek and smiled."

"The Lieutenant was sweaty and nervous. I turned around and took the hands of the boys and began the final steps to the sea. As I turned my back on the soldiers and began to walk away I heard the Lieutenant call the order, 'Take your aim, Ready...' Then there was silence. I turned around and saw the Lieutenant drop his rifle and fall to the sand in tears. He wept. I let go of the boys' arms and walked back to the Lieutenant. I bent down and wiped away his tears. I said, 'I love you.' And as these words left my mouth, I could hear the joyful screams and laughter of the boys as they raced onto the beach and touched the holy water of the ocean. I stayed with the Lieutenant and comforted him."

Holy people like Bishop Tutu walk among us and live lives of spiritual practices each and every day. Yes, they do great things. Great things that maybe you and I are not ready or prepared to do yet. But I promise you this: Each of them started out on a spiritual path by doing the smallest of things. They continually experience the holy in the simplest acts of life. True spirituality and spiritual practice require action. True spirituality seeks participation in social justice for the entire human family.

Developing spirituality and spiritual practices are not only done in private. It would not be very spiritual if it were only for your own benefit. The ultimate goal of developing yourself spiritually is to express it in some public action. The great spiritual teachers invite all of us not only to partake in daily spiritual practices, but also have the courage to do so publicly.

Animals

"I think I could turn and live with the animals,
they are so placid and self-contain'd.
I stand and look at them long and long.
They do not sweat and whine about their
condition,
They do not lie awake in the dark and weep
for their sins,
They do not make me sick discussing their
duty to God,
Not one is dissatisfied, not one is demented
with the mania of owning things,
Not one kneels to another, nor to his kind
that lived thousands of years ago,
Not one is respectable or unhappy over
the whole earth."
—WALT WHITMAN

WITH THE URBANIZATION of our world, we have become separated from the intimate interaction experienced between humans and animals. Nevertheless, we are experiencing a renewal of respect for animals in our culture. Throughout the country, state and local governments are enacting new laws, protecting animals from abuse and neglect and providing strict punishments for those who violate these laws.

Even before the written word existed, we find powerful sacred images of the spiritual connection between animals and human beings. This idea is portrayed in petroglyph cave paintings, in statues and carvings from the pyramids of the pharaohs, and in artifacts unearthed around the globe.

In times past, we experienced animals as teachers, guardians, and invaluable partners in life. We are now awakening to ask ourselves the question, what is our relationship with the animal world?

A New Reverence for Animals

THE SURVIVAL OF THE HUMAN RACE—our spiritual, physical, and cultural survival—depends on our relationship with animals. The deep ecology movement that has emerged as a new science shows that a profound respect for animals and our environment is necessary for the continued function of our planet.

Modern research has shown that living with pets provides health benefits. Science is proving that our relationship with animals has a physical, healing effect. Elderly pet owners visit doctors less often than those without pets. A study from Dr. Karen Allen at the State University of New York at Buffalo found that owning a cat or dog can lower your blood pressure or ward off depression. It improves survival rates after suffering a heart attack, and it cuts down on the number of visits to your doctor. Australian researchers found that male pet owners have lower cholesterol levels. The University of California at Davis School of Veterinary Medicine shows Alzheimer's patients have fewer outbursts if there is an animal in the home. Midland Life Insurance Company of Columbus, Ohio asks clients over the age of 75 if they have a pet, giving pet owners preferential treatment when they are looking for life or long-term-care insurance.

Animals function in many different ways in our world today. They are going with us into nursing homes and hospitals to facilitate healing. They are used therapeutically with troubled children and people who have experienced severe traumas. They are important as companions. Then there are the animals that work for a living. Drug dogs, bomb dogs, cadaver dogs, seeing-eye dogs and ponies are providing huge benefits to humans.

Animals can lead us on a deeper journey in life, physically, emotionally and spiritually.

Spiritual Lessons of Animals

WHEN WE LOOK AT ANIMALS, the qualities that we admire in them are most likely things we desire within ourselves. Eastern traditions treat animals within mystic structures. In the Native American culture, animals are experienced as totems—symbols of specific attributes such as the turtle for patience, the horse for power, the butterfly for transformation, and the dog for loyalty.

Some of us experience animals as the presence of angels in our midst. Let's not forget, often our first experience of life and death as children was with the death of our animals. None of us can forget the pure and simple, but amazingly powerful experience of our first pet. Animals exude virtues only experienced in the realms of saints and angels as they display humility, loyalty, unselfishness, forgiveness, happiness, playfulness, and a profound sense of peace.

When you greet your pet look intentionally into their eyes, smile, and ask a blessing upon them. You may say, "Bless you my friend" or "God bless you." Be creative with your good wish for your companion. Make sure you give thanks to your pet for their life and sharing your journey together. You will love this practice and your pet will love it, too. In this moment you are fully present with your pet.

Animals remind us each day about the joy of the simple things in life: that we are not alone, but part of a larger significant community of all life in this world.

Gardening

"Cultivate peace and harmony."
—GEORGE WASHINGTON

GARDENING HAS BEEN an integral part of the human experience throughout recorded history. Murals of vegetables were painted on ancient tombs depicting their importance. In Europe, famous explorers brought back fruits and vegetables from the new lands they conquered all over the world. They kept detailed records of the plants found in their travels. Seeds were considered sacred and handed down like jewels from generation to generation. As we settled new lands, one of the most sacred objects we carried with us were our seeds. There is a tremendous reverence for plants and gardens in the early teachings of all religions. From monasteries to palaces, all had gardens that connected them to the Divine.

As a result of the Industrial Revolution, we methodically became disconnected from the earth. We saw the introduction of canned fruits and vegetables. The storage of food became institutionalized.

In recent years, there has been an almost revolutionary return to the earth. Now more than ever, people are eating fresh and raw vegetables. There is not a restaurant you can go into that does not feature health-conscious items on the menu. Medical experts recommend fresh fruit and vegetables as a mainstay in our diet as a source of anti-oxidants. We see fresh flowers in our homes, plants in our offices. The teachings of bonsai, Ikebana, and feng shui are bringing the art of the garden back into our popular culture. In every aspect of our society today, there is an inspired return to the earth through gardening.

Spiritual Imagery of Gardening

THE METAPHORS FOR OUR SPIRITUAL LIFE are grounded in gardening: seeds, planting, watering, growth. Gardening is a constant reminder of the cycle of life and death. The seed is given life by the earth. It grows, creates abundance through the nourishment of water and food, and eventually returns to the earth in its death. We learn from the seasons as well, seeing new life in spring, the fullness of life in summer, shedding and surrender in fall, and peace and stillness in winter.

Gardening leads us to the spiritual practice of tending. We have reverence for the potential of the seed. We practice trust and surrender as we drop a seed into the mystery of the darkness of the soil. It teaches us waiting and patience. It teaches us about loss, hope, joy, gratitude, success, and failure. There has always been the image of Mother Earth. Again, we see the life cycle arising from her and returning to her. Gardening teaches us reverence for the food chain, it teaches the interconnectedness of all life.

For many, the Garden of Eden was the beginning of the human race. Buddha performed his teachings in the garden under the bodhi tree. Jesus prayed in the Garden of Gethsemane. Moses was in a garden, when the bush began to burn. Hindus still worship their gods with gifts from the earth.

As Thich Nhat Hanh says, "Earth brings us into life and nourishes us. Earth takes us back again. Birth and death are present in every moment."

Your Green Thumb

THERE ARE MANY LESSONS you can learn in gardening. It is an exercise in awareness. Observe the plant and in awareness see if it lacks water, if it lacks light, is diseased, or needs new earth. In developing awareness with a garden, develop an inner awareness with yourself. This awareness forces you to live in the present moment. When you live in the present moment you can experience the fullness of joy, peace, and serenity.

Having plants is an exercise in balance. The balance of the elements in a garden reflects the balance in your own life. A garden leads you into the experience of trust because you are trusting in the life cycle—the cycle of Nature. As this trust develops, your reverence for your connection to the earth continues to grow.

You don't necessarily have to have a large garden like our grandparents did in years past. You can go to the garden center and get one tomato plant or one flower for your patio or yard. What is important is experiencing the process of growth and change and seeing how it reflects in your life.

Many of us live in urban areas or are too busy to experience a garden. But you can still experience the thrill of gardening by purchasing plants and fresh fruits and vegetables on a regular basis. The local fresh-air market or garden center has the possibility of becoming your surrogate garden. Create a garden by putting a plant in your kitchen window, by your bathtub, on your desk, or in the bud vase of your car.

Whatever you do, connect yourself back to nature. Connect yourself back to the earth, your mother.

Leisure

"One day a hunter in the desert saw Abba
Anthony enjoying himself with the brethren and he was
shocked. What kind of spiritual guide was this?

But the old monk said to him, 'Put an arrow in your
bow and shoot it.' So the hunter did. Then the old man
said, 'Now shoot another.' And the hunter did. Then
the elder said, 'Shoot your bow again. Keep shooting;
keep shooting; keep shooting.' And the hunter finally
said, 'But if I bend my bow so much I will break it.'

Then Abba Anthony said to him, 'It is just the same
with the work of God. If we stretch ourselves beyond
measure, we will break. Sometimes it is necessary to
meet other needs.' When the hunter heard these words
he was struck with remorse and, greatly edified by Anthony, he went away. As for the monastics there, they
went home strengthened." —THE DESERT FATHERS

ONE OF THE LEAST ACCEPTED spiritual practices
in America today is the ancient practice of leisure.
Leisure has two aspects: play and rest. Even Abba
Anthony in the second century was warning people about

the critical role of leisure. Leisure is all about balance. Our society's skewing of time is completely off balance. Nature created balance with day and night. But with the advent of electricity and human-created light sources, we can and do continue to work later and later into the night. Balance with our families is becoming harder and harder as well. As a consequence our souls are drying up. We need to heed the lesson of Abba Anthony, taking time from our work to play and rest.

Americans have forgotten how to play and rest. We are the hardest working nation in the world. We glorify work and workaholics. This has thrust our society terribly out of balance. Remember the image of the teeter totter on the playground? One person on one end and one on the other: This is a lesson in balance. For both people to have the fullest experience on the teeter totter you had to stay in constant balance. Our bodies are depleted and exhausted from how hard we are working. So are our souls.

Spiritual Ramifications

LEISURE IS AN ESSENTIAL PART of our spirituality. Leisure is one of the most difficult spiritual practices to achieve, because we are doers and makers, not dreamers and reflectors. We do not teach people to reflect on what they do.

The concept of Sabbath, or rest, is in all major world religions. Sabbath is not about God needing rest. It is about teaching *us* to rest. The Talmud teaches three reasons why the Sabbath is critical: It equalizes rich and poor; it gives us time to evaluate our work to see if it is good; and it gives us time to contemplate the meaning of life. The book of Genesis tells us that after the work of creation, God stopped and rested from all work. Rest was such a revered practice that God blessed the experience of rest.

Isn't it sad that in our society we teach everyone to work, but we don't teach them to play? Play was the basis of leisure time throughout all societies. The function of holy days and festivals was to provide all levels of people the opportunity to play and celebrate together. It was an opportunity to equalize social classes through leisure.

Leisure is for holy things; it engages the heart and stretches the soul.

On the Playground of Life

LEISURE IS NOT A VACATION FROM LIFE, rather it brings meaning to your life because it allows you the time to contemplate. Leisure is not withdrawal from the human race: It is essential to the health and happiness of the human race. Work becomes more meaningful and has a purpose when we experience leisure.

Relearn play and rest. Now is the time to explore and discover new ways to play and to rest. There are a variety of ways to commune with Nature in both play and rest. Be creative. Explore new possibilities. Make it fun. Explore your city. There are so many things going on that you may not think about: museum openings, art festivals, free concerts, zoos, historical sites. The Internet is a great resource for finding current activities in your neighborhood.

For your rest time, take a nap. We have science that shows the health benefits of a good nap. Go sit under a tree like when you were a child. Lay in your yard or in a park with your children or by yourself and discover the shapes hiding in the clouds. Rediscover yourself on the playground and never, ever lose that joy in your life again.

Music

---

*"If you cannot teach me to fly,
teach me to sing."*—SIR JAMES BARRIE

FOR THOUSANDS OF YEARS people have recognized the power of music. Some of the earliest music—drumming and horns—was used for communications. These sounds told of invaders approaching or strangers infiltrating. Music is a source of vital connection to one's self and others. Music—with no words—at times can be more intimate that the most eloquent lyrics. Music crosses all cultures, nations, races, denominations. It is the most genuine, flawless, and authentic form of communication. Music is food for the body and soul.

There are different forms of music: music with instruments, orchestral music, and bands. We have people singing with choral music. Chanting is a very ancient form of music. And there are the different genres of music evolving everyday. Music is a path that leads us deeper into ourselves, our communities, and a presence greater than ourselves.

Reasons Behind Rhythms

A STUDY FROM THE UNIVERSITY OF WASHINGTON showed that a group of workers listening to music increased productivity over 21 percent. Many corporations have found that music can increase efficiency, cut training time, and increase output.

Restaurants play music because it stimulates digestion. A Michigan State University study showed that listening to music for only 15 minutes increased the blood's level of Interluken-1—a family of proteins associated with blood and platelet production and cellular protection against AIDS, cancer, and many other diseases. *The Journal of the American Medical Association* reported a study that found that half the mothers who listened to music during childbirth did not require anesthesia. Hearing is the first sense that develops in utero.

Music is a medium of connection across cultural divides. It lets us communicate beyond language barriers. We may not know what is being said, but we can perceive the message on a level beyond words. Music is also culturally defined. We may be in Asia, South America, or Africa and know immediately where we are by the music being played. Think about Disney's Epcot Center where they indicate what nation you are visiting by changing the soundtrack!

Music has an immediate effect on our emotions and the chemicals in our bodies that are released from the brain. Music increases endorphin levels—the brain's opiates—thus creating a natural high. A scientist at Stanford found in a recent study that half his subjects experienced euphoria while listening to music. The exhilaration the music produced is the result of stimulating the pituitary gland which increases electrical activity in the brain.

Music may be the key to open many new experiences. Many of us need physical, psychological or emotional healing. You may desire new inspiration, productivity and creativity in your life. Music has astounding transformational power and is beckoning you at this very moment.

Who Could Ask for Anything More?

MUSIC IS AN INVITATION to explore the mystery that is dancing within your soul. Be aware of what you are attracted to and what repels you when you listen. Experiment with different forms of music in our culture and with music from other cultures. Explore the spiritual side of music. You may want to visit a drumming circle, or learn the spiritual and physical attributes of chanting.

If you have always wanted to sing and have never felt comfortable with your voice, purchase a karaoke machine. Have a karaoke night and sing your heart out. Or, put music on in your car that you love and sing along.

History has told us, academic institutions have told us, science has told us, healers and shamans have told us, the power of music is limitless.

Supper

"One cannot think well, love well, sleep well, if one has not dined well."—VIRGINIA WOOLF

OR MANY OF US, the concept of feasting is foreign and forgotten. We have drifted into a time when many of us experience our evening meal as a mundane, nondescript event. It has simply become another exhausting task at the end of an already overwhelming day. Dining has been relegated to a prefabricated ritual that has lost all its reverence in our modern society with all its modern conveniences. Many of us experience our daily meals as fast food; take-out food, food in a bag, dehydrated food, food in the freezer, instant food.

When the way we experience food becomes instant, we have to be careful that we do not lose the reverence for the toil of farm hands, and suffer a separation from Mother Nature herself. Technology has blessed our families with convenience, but we must be cautious that this does not drive us further and further away from our grounding in the earth. The core of the human experience is the transformation of raw ingredients into mental, physical, emotional and spiritual nourishment and sustenance. It is time to reclaim this.

It is important to stop once in a while and take time for food. You must attempt, on occasion, to make food a feast. This is especially important if you have children in your home.

The current trend of remodeling kitchens and filling them with gadgets and gizmos is our attempt to reconnect with how things used to be. We remember the comfort and joy of eating and cooking in the kitchens of our mothers and grandmothers. We realize that the kitchen can be a gathering place for our families even today. The kitchen is the new living room, the social area of the house, the primary entertainment venue for the home. It has the potential to become the place where family and religious rituals are celebrated. Intimate conversations are carried deep into the night and the hearts and souls of those gathered there are inextricably woven together.

Time and convenience are important in today's world. But that doesn't mean that the feast should not tantalize all of our senses and become a fully sensual experience. Eating is both a physical and spiritual experience.

Return to the Sacred

ALL SPIRITUAL TRADITIONS share the feast ritual. Judaism has Shabbat and Seder; Christianity has Holy Communion. Islam celebrates the Feast of Eid Al-Fitr, marking the end of the fast of Ramadan. In Buddhism and Taoism, reverence is shown for the gods through food offerings. And Hindus feed their gods fruits, milk, nuts, and other food items. There are countless meals through the various faiths associated with holidays, rites, and rituals.

Religious traditions also have customs about the types of foods consumed and the methods by which food is prepared. Catholicism historically excluded the partaking of meat on Fridays and certain holy days. Traditionally, Jews eat kosher food that is prepared according to a code of strict dietary laws that provide, among other things, that meat and dairy products must be prepared separately and must not be eaten together. Fish with both fins and scales may be eaten, but not shellfish. Buddhists do not generally eat meat at all. And where many Hindus avoid beef, neither Muslims nor Jews consume pork.

In many cultures there is an emphasis on intention and emotion in cooking. The simplest meal can be the healthiest food in the world if prepared in a spirit of affection and goodwill. The *Bagavhad Gita*—a sacred Hindu scripture—teaches that the intention of the cook is actually transferred to the food. The loving cook strengthens the power of each food whereas an unhappy cook creates food with little nourishment.

The Mindful Feast

WHY NOT TRY TO REDISCOVER the authenticity of preparing and enjoying food? Not just eating the chocolate cake, but the wonderful process of preparing it: mixing the ingredients and licking the beaters. Let's try *being* in the kitchen, and not just doing in the kitchen.

Challenge yourself and your family to eat intentionally once a week. It can be a spiritual experience to commune over your food. If you live in a family situation it is significant when all participate in the family meal. If you live alone, attempt to share a meal once a week with someone, a friend or a neighbor, and maybe even consider creating a meal-time family.

Develop mindfulness in your cooking. It is a perfect time to tap into your creativity: crafting with colors, textures, the origin of foods. There has never been a better time for making food choices. Consider where your food is grown. Is your food homegrown? Is it organic? A part of having reverence for food is making intelligent decisions about your food. It is important not to pass judgment on foods that are from the freezer or are easily prepared. Companies like Bird's Eye have developed techniques that capture more of the nutritional value of the food than you might find sitting around at a local farm stand. National growers meet tougher FDA standards than local farmers.

Light a candle, use silverware, cotton napkins, china, put flowers on your table. These are things you can do out of reverence for the meal. Turn off the TV, put down the newspaper.

Bless your food. Begin by gazing at your food: create an attitude of gratefulness. Become aware of the colors on your plate, the table, and the people gathered. Breathe in and out slowly three times, smile, and enjoy the connection with your food.

Create a personal blessing that acknowledges the process by which your food came to your table, your gratefulness for the sacrifices others have made for your meal and your gratitude for having enough to eat. Pause and mindfully look at your food before you put it in your mouth.

If you consider your meal a mindful process, you begin to develop a healthier relationship with your food. From all our experiences food is inextricably linked with relationships. And relationships are the core of spirituality. Taking a few extra intentional minutes at meal time is one of the easiest ways to turn an everyday activity into a spiritually rewarding experience.

Washing the Dishes

"Confine yourself to the present."
—MARCUS AURELIUS

WHAT IS MORE EVERYDAY than washing the dishes? For many of us it is the standard family punishment or the trade-off for not cooking. In truth, washing the dishes is part of the ritual cycle of food. If you don't finish the dishes, you are not finishing the cycle, which must be done in order to start the ritual again.

Holy Dishwashers

BROTHER LAWRENCE was a Carmelite brother who lived in France during the seventeenth century. His spiritual counsel was simple: throughout every day, keep an ongoing conversation with God. He joyfully scrubbed the pots of his monastery in order to see the face of God in his reflection under the grime of the day's meal. Even today, Buddhist monk Thich Nhat Hanh uses washing dishes as a practice in prayer and meditation.

How To

THE REASON THAT YOU WANT to develop washing the dishes as a spiritual practice is simple. If you have to stand there for 15–20 minutes doing this mundane chore, you might as well use it as a joyful meditative experience rather than an exhaustive task. It truly becomes a choice. Instead of the time being hurried and unpleasant, you can create a sacred time when you are joyful. You can accompany this practice by focusing on your breath, listening to music, singing, or chanting. This time of dishwashing can also be as important as a time of meditation or prayer.

Doing the dishes can be a time of developing deeper relationships in the family. One person can wash the dishes and the other can dry. In that short period of time, you can share conversation and gain wonderful, pure family time.

Cleaning up can be a time for silence and meditation. It can be a time for laughter and sharing. However you approach it, you will soon quit dreading doing the dishes.

CHAPTER FOUR

Metamorphosis

AS I BEGAN TO DRIVE OFF I noticed my sleeve was ripped open. There was blood down my arm and my pant legs were covered with it. I had been so busy there was no time to notice anything at all. I wondered whose blood it was. Was it the baby's or the toddler's? I don't think it was the man's because that was seeping from his ears, nose, and mouth. I couldn't remember touching him there. But it all happened so fast anything was possible.

It was a sultry Sunday afternoon in Georgia. I was returning from a spiritual director's certification program that I had been working on for two years. I had finally finished a long period of writing papers, spending time in the required supervision sessions, and was now on my way home from my last residency for the program. I was excited that I had finished and I was now a certified Spiritual Director.

Tricia Yearwood was singing to me on the radio down this long boring highway, when all of a sudden the car in front of me went out of control. It began swerving then started rolling over and over until it finally stopped on the side of the road in a swampy area. I immediately called 911 and pulled off the road. The car had landed upright and I saw two heads in the front seat, but no one was moving. I ran over, but it was difficult getting close because the car was firmly planted in the mud. The first thing I saw was a man with the steering wheel crushing into his chest. There was blood all over his face. He was unconscious. In the passenger seat was a woman covered with glass, also unconscious. I heard a rustling in the back seat and there on the floor board were two children. Both were awake and the baby began to cry. The children were covered with blood.

The back seat car doors wouldn't open. But the glass was broken out of the windows. I reached in and grabbed the infant first. She was bleeding from surface glass cuts. One gash was deep. I noticed a package of disposable diapers on the seat and grabbed one to apply pressure on the wound. At this point several cars had stopped. A man was standing at the side of the road. I ran to him with the infant in my arms and told him to hold the baby and keep the pressure on the wound. I ran back and grabbed the toddler who was now standing up on the back seat. She was bleeding from her arm and her head. Again, I snatched her, applied some more disposable diapers to her wounds, and handed her to another man on the side of the road.

As I approached the car this time, the woman on the passenger's side had become conscious. I tried to open her door to pull her from the car. But the mud made it impossible. For the first time I noticed that none of the people who had stopped were helping me drag these people from the car.

It was at that moment I noticed the smell of gasoline. I looked down and gas was bubbling up in the mud surrounding the car. I was covered up to my waist with a concoction of mud and fuel. I refused to allow myself to think about the possibilities of the steaming car engine and the pooling gasoline. I focused on the children's mother. I will never forget how heavy that woman was. She was twice as big as I was but I was determined to get her out of that car. I pulled and I prayed. I pulled and I prayed. I pulled harder and I prayed more. She was finally free from the car and then came the most difficult part, dragging her through the mud and gasoline. It was a miracle that I finally got her to the side of the road. She was in shock. I was afraid she had internal injuries. I remembered that my suitcase was in my trunk, so I raced to my trunk and grabbed some clothing. A man helped me cover the woman as she lay by the side of the road.

I had been so busy, I hadn't noticed that no emergency personnel had arrived yet. We were in a desolate area. Where were they? I hurried back to the wrecked car. There was this pitiful man trapped in the car under the steering wheel. I crawled into the passenger side of the car and began to talk to him. He floated in and out of consciousness. I tried to encourage and assure him that help was on the way. I knew he was dying, there was blood coming from everywhere. The tears started to stream down his face as he whispered, "Please don't leave me, I'm scared." I sat beside him and held his hand. I promised him that I would sit right by him and pray until somebody came to cut him out of the car. I wasn't going anywhere. In the meantime, dozens of people had stopped on the side of the interstate, but no one came close to the car.

Finally, the ambulances, police and helicopters arrived, and carried this precious family off to the hospitals in Atlanta. As I slowly walked to my car, I approached the people that had watched, but never offered to help. I walked up to them and asked them, "Why didn't you help me?" They looked at each other. One answered, "I am a teacher and when I saw the blood, I didn't have any plastic gloves so I wasn't going to touch anyone." The next one said, "I am a broker, I didn't know what to do. You acted like a doctor, so I just watched." The final man responded, "I thought you were a doctor, too. I didn't think I could help because I am a minister."

I drove off and gazed in my review mirror. It was quite a scene. The interstate was closed down. Helicopters littered the highway carrying off bodies. I just wondered: why wouldn't anyone help me? Was it because of all the blood? Was it because of the danger of the gasoline? Was it because it was blatantly obvious that these people were poor? They were driving a rattle trap of a car. The children had no clothes on and were only in diapers. They were black. Please God, tell me it didn't have to do with their poverty and their race. I'll never know, but I always wonder.

Opportunity Knocks

WHATEVER OPPORTUNITIES APPEAR in your life—great or small—you are equipped to deal with them when you are grounded in your own spiritual practices. Over time, your spiritual practices will prepare you for a life beyond your greatest expectations. Over time, these spiritual practices transform you and you literally become new. An astonishing metamorphosis occurs in your mind, body and soul. Your life not only becomes more meaningful, but you may discover a new purpose for your life that you were never aware of before.

One of my greatest mentors has been His Holiness, the fourteenth Dalai Lama. I have had the opportunity to study with His Holiness and listen to his wisdom, humor and love. It is impossible to sit in his presence and not be in awe of the manner in which he experiences life. This man lived through the slaughter and horrors of the communist takeover of his homeland of Tibet. He barely escaped with his own life. No matter how life has challenged him, he sees potential, love, and possibility in the experience.

As he reflected on his leaving Nepal and living in exile in India, the Dalai Lama views his exile as a good thing. He believes that the world now knows more about Buddhism because of his public posture. He has become the spokesperson and the incarnation of the tenants of Buddhism. His Holiness embodies compassion, love, and forgiveness. He surrendered to his horrible circumstances, continued with his spiritual practices throughout the turmoil that raged in his life, and has experienced metamorphosis. He has shifted from a Dalai Lama in remote Tibet to a global figure that has continued to give the world hope. In the midst of a world embroiled in war, violence, and greed he preaches peace, love, nonviolence, forgiveness, and compassion. He has become a dominant voice in the world for peace.

Why did I choose this particular story when talking about metamorphosis? When you first become aware that there is an opportunity to live in a new way, for the rest of your life, a choice immediately emerges. The choice becomes clear. It asks, can I surrender to something new and in that surrender experience my life as infinite possibilities? Or, do I continue to orchestrate and direct my life to include what I want to experience and isolate any experience that may tax me or make me feel uncomfortable?

If you choose to surrender to the life of infinite possibilities, then you have chosen the road less traveled. When you choose this path, it is important to underpin your life with spiritual practices to give you strength and courage for your journey. Without exception, all of the extraordinary people that have been woven into my life—Jimmy Carter, Desmond Tutu, the Dalai Lama, Thich Nhat Hanh, Mother Teresa, and so many more—all maintain daily spiritual practices. They keep themselves ready for the bumps in the road of life. Their greatness has evolved from their simple daily practices.

There is an old saying that goes something like this: "The person who prizes the smallest things in life is surely worthy of the great ones." I promise you this: As you practice acts of awareness, breathing, living mindfully and compassionately, you will experience metamorphosis. The gift of spirituality is that you can participate in life in a much more substantial and meaningful way. This is the reward of embracing spirituality: full participation in the world on many levels, emotional, physical, intellectual and spiritual.

The Evening News

"Current events are so grim that we often can't decide whether or not we dare to watch the six o'clock news."—ANONYMOUS

---

*H*AVE YOU STOPPED WATCHING the evening news? You shouldn't have. You should watch the news in order to stay informed about what is going on in the world. You can watch the news, just do it with a different mindset.

There are ways you may want to explore to create a new understanding of the news. You can listen so that it doesn't appear to be a daily version of the Armageddon story. Whether it is the scarcity of water, the melting of the polar icecaps, or the constant threat of terrorism, the underlying theme is one of what's the world coming to? And, we are living in the end times. Much of the news has been placed into the larger context of despair and hopelessness. In fact, there is little basis for such despair.

We respond to this constant threat of Armageddon in several ways. Some of us reject the argument and live in anger. Others accept it and live in fear. Others live in apathy, denying that they have any power at all and choose indiscriminate resignation.

The End is Not Near

THIS END-TIMES PHILOSOPHY IS NOT NEW. Think about Nostradamus in the sixteenth century. Every ten or fifteen years, one of his predictions surfaces, signaling that it is time for the end of the world. For several years before the year 2000, we had Y2K that created a multi-million dollar industry in books, seminars, and supplies to prepare us for the end of the world.

Armageddon peddlers have created a spiritual practice based on the idea of an in group, the out group, and the chosen ones. Fear is traded as a commodity and has been transformed into a political strategy. It's unsettling that a select few have created this mythical frenzy and have cashed in on fortunes through deliberate misinformation.

No One's Left Behind

HOW DO YOU KEEP CURRENT EVENTS from deadening your spirits? How do you watch the news without being trapped in the web of underlying doom? You can begin by watching the news objectively. Be aware of catch phrases, listen for charged words, watch the manipulation of language. Develop a spiritual practice that when you watch, you decide if the news is based in reality or sensationalism.

You can develop spiritual practices to keep from being negatively affected by the news. Compassionately look at the facts, detach yourself from them, and be sympathetic to those involved. Put the people concerned in this or that event on your prayer list. When you hear of a horrible accident or a convenience store robbery, pray for all the people involved—the victims, the police and emergency personnel, even the perpetrators who will be held responsible for their actions.

Instead of being victimized by the event, become empowered and commit yourself to some action. Put spiritual practice into action. There is an old axiom that goes: "If you are not part of the solution, you are part of the problem." When you participate in the world you become part of the solution that heals the plague of apathy in our country.

Family

"*The greatest institution in the world
is the human family.*"—ANONYMOUS

COMMUNITY IS A MANDATE from the Divine. And, fortunately, the structure of our society provides instant communities for us in the form of families. Relationships are essential. Nothing has greater impact on health than love and relationships. The University of Michigan published a landmark paper that demonstrated people without strong social support were two to four times more likely to die than those with substantial social networks.

TV's *Late Night with David Letterman Show* and others like it are consciously designed as family models with the father, the son, the wacky uncle all playing their parts. This structure is something we are familiar and comfortable with.

The family is deeply and significantly engrained in us as it is our first layer of social relationships.

A New View of Family

FAMILY CAN BE BEST DEFINED as a household—people living under the same roof. This does not have to be bound to the traditional model of mom, dad, and kids. Then again, family does not necessarily have to be in the same location. By maintaining close relationships and regular contact we can create a family.

Family has an extended definition and the family image is one of constant change. Family is a dynamic idea that we are continuously redefining because we have to.

While we may believe that this flexible idea of the family is new, it in fact is not. The founders of major religions displayed this in their lives. Christ, Buddha, Mohammad, Moses, all created a family of disciples.

The concept of the family has now expanded to the notion of one human family. One of the greatest reminders and reinforcements of this idea is the horrors of 9/11 and how all people—stockbrokers, rescue workers, janitors—joined together as a global family in the face of crisis. Hopefully, what we have learned from the horrors of 9/11 is that we can reach out and create families anywhere, anytime, any place.

I'll Be There for You

MANY OF US ARE BORN into families. But we all have the privilege and the abilities to choose families. Look for opportunities to create families in your life, as they are all around you. Create a family around a book club, a project, the military, an association, a cause, a religious group. Even if you live alone, you have the potential to create your own family with animals, plants, neighbors, and friends. You can create your family at work.

A family can be the most fertile place for spiritual development. Families are the container, the vehicle, the petri dish for our growth potential. Inside the family people experience the raw vulnerability of you. Therein lies its power.

The Donna Reed Show and *Leave It to Beaver* were historical television representations of family. This experience of family was rigid, static, boxed within the suburbanization of the country. There is now fluidity in family. We now have *Friends* and *Will & Grace* redefining our modern notions of family, teaching us that biology is not what is important, but rather love, support, and relationship.

Intimacy

"We can be intimate with flowers, animals,
trees, and stars, and can be nourished
by the experience. But the most powerful
and profound awareness of ourselves
occurs with our simultaneous opening up
with another human."—PAT MALONE

WHAT DO YOU THINK of when you hear the word "intimacy"? You may pause and listen more intensely. You may look with an eye of suspicion. Or like many of us, you may sigh with a feeling of being overwhelmed—just one more thing to do. I believe that if you ask a hundred people the definition of intimacy, most of them would say it has to do with sex. Let's challenge ourselves to expand the definition of intimacy beyond the sexual context. Instead let's consider intimacy as closeness, familiarity, affection, understanding, and connection—not exclusively with others, but with ourselves as well. It is intimacy with ourselves that is most significant and important as it is impossible to have intimacy with another person if you don't have it with yourself first.

Intimacy is primarily how you see into yourself. Secondarily, it is how others experience you. It is an act of great courage to intentionally want to see who you really are. It requires vulnerability and surrender to achieve intimacy. When you give yourself permission to see into yourself, what you find may allow you a deeper, more profound, connection with yourself, with the Divine, and with others.

Intimacy, like food and shelter, is one of the basic human needs.

Intimacy Heals

THERE ARE MANY SCIENTIFIC STUDIES correlating the significance of intimacy with health. According to Dr. Dean Ornish, "Love and intimacy are at the root of what makes us sick and what makes us well, what causes sadness, and what brings happiness, what makes us suffer and what leads to healing. If a new drug had the same impact, virtually every doctor in the country would be recommending it to their patients. It would be malpractice not to prescribe it."

What is stopping you from experiencing intimacy? There may be a variety of reasons. Many emotions like depression, anger, or fear cause disconnects in our relationships with ourselves and others. These emotions can cause us to withdraw. A numbness can develop in our bodies and souls. Intimacy may seem impossible. Sleep deprivation or insomnia also inhibit intimacy. When we are exhausted, it is almost impossible to muster the energy to be intimate. Stress—the worldwide epidemic of today—creates a state of worry within us. We worry about what happened yesterday and what will happen tomorrow. We rob ourselves of the present and there is no possibility for intimacy.

A problem with intimacy is even though our technology allows us to communicate faster and more often, it does not mean you experience greater intimacy. With cell phones, e-mails, and beepers we are not physically in the presence of another person. Our culture teaches us to go forward, to move faster. But intimacy is a movement inward. Intimacy is a spiral moving inward toward the inner you.

We are disconnected, absent and truly not present in the hurriedness of our lives today. We are distracted, preoccupied and exhausted.

Experience Intimacy

THE JOURNEY BACK to our intimate self is not an event, it is a process. It is a process that takes your intention to create intimacy in your life. If intimacy has been missing from your life for a long time, it won't return overnight. Intimacy is like a muscle that needs to be exercised and cared for on a regular basis.

The primary practice to employ to reach intimacy is awareness. Turn off the distractions: radios, televisions, computers, cell phones, beepers. All of these wonderful technological tools create motion, movement, and distraction in our souls. Imagine this as an adventure into the full, vulnerable, sensual, creative you.

Explore intimacy through your senses. Smells, touch, sounds, tastes, images. Let's begin with Nature. If you love the ocean, imagine the ocean breeze on the skin of your body, the smell and feel of salt. Experience the thrill and awe of the sunset or the sunrise over the water.

You may enjoy rain more. As the rain surrounds you, imagine the smell, the sound, the feel. There are innumerable possibilities to experience a primal sense of intimacy in Nature: the silence of a fresh snow; a summer night echoing with the sound of crickets; or the midnight sky scattered with bright stars. Nature is a powerful ally on your path to intimacy.

Animals are a profound source of intimacy. They consistently gift us with love and faithful companionship. If you have lost touch with your intimate self, try lying down beside your dog or cat and in the silence be aware of the connection between you and the animal. The natural intimacy of animals calls us to mirror them and become intimate ourselves.

There is nothing like a great book to capture you in another time and place, where you can undergo a myriad of emotions and relationships within the pages at your fingertips. Sitting on the back porch wrapped in a down comforter, you can experience intimacy with yourself, with the characters, with the scenes of your book.

When you find yourself becoming numb or lost, why not try pulling out your favorite movie? Find some movies you love that lead you home to yourself. They are a trusted friend.

Finally, develop your own sacred intimate practices. Create rituals that make you feel loved, nurtured, and appreciated. Try designing your own tea ceremony, a sensual bath, or a restoring nap.

There are many doors that are available to you to open and see into your self. There are many windows to the soul. Nature, water, music, art, a pet—all of these have the potential for engaging the senses and thus creating a greater intimacy with yourself and others.

While not exclusive to intimacy, if you feel that depression, anxiety or insomnia are keeping you from intimacy or limiting you in any other way from fully experiencing your life, you may want to explore some of the practices mentioned above. If meditation, prayer, yoga, or other exercises are not helping you with your depression, anxiety, or insomnia, you may want to consult a physician. There are remarkable medicines available on the market today that are helping people live healthier, more productive lives. You can try different methods to help yourself or ask a professional for help, but there is no reason for you to suffer.

Intimacy, in all its many forms, is a part of your life. Intimacy should not be quantified by a specific time, with a specific person, at a specific place. True, authentic, intimacy can be experienced in your everyday activities.

Bath

---

*"There must be quite a few things
a hot bath won't cure, but I don't know
many of them."*—SYLVIA PLATH

---

*I*F YOU ARE A MAN, you don't get it or you don't care. If you are a woman, the bath represents and signifies everything you know about the word sanctuary.

A study from the Sleep Disorders Clinic at Stanford University found bathing helpful in the treatment of sleep disorders. When your body gets ready for sleep, your body temperature drops. A bath reduces your body temperature and nudges your bedtime biochemistry along. In 2000, a Harris Interactive poll found that 100 percent of the 2,000 women interviewed found baths relaxing. Sixty percent said they would be happier if they could take a bath every day. We remember bathing as babies and kids. It's not unusual to see a picture of children playing in the bathtub. We remember the bath being a playful time, a time of giggling and spontaneity. We were thrilled with our nakedness.

Because of the fast-paced world we live in, there has been a revival in finding ways to relax and nestle in our homes. The greatest amount of home improvement money today is spent on building and renovating bathrooms. While the size of our bedrooms is staying the same, the size of our bathrooms is growing. This shows a profound desire for us to seek nurturing and serenity. While we appreciate the bath in Western culture, we have largely lost the deeper meaning and spiritual connection with the art of bathing.

Communion

THE BATH IS A RELAXATION RITUAL. We find ourselves concentrating on the function, not the experience of the bath. We are not taking enough time for the bath.

The central art of bathing has underpinned many cultures. In Roman times, people lounging around baths was an essential element of their culture. In Japan, communal baths were a social event. Baths have traditionally been used for medicinal purposes as well. We continually find ancient stories of baths being used with salts and oils for healing various maladies. U.S. President Franklin D. Roosevelt used the natural warm springs near his summer home in Georgia as a treatment for his polio. Even today, baths are prescribed by health care professionals for a variety of ailments.

Water has always symbolized purification and release in all spiritualities and religious traditions. For Christians, baptism; for Hindus, purification in the River Ganges; for Jews, *mikva*, a communal bath for ritual cleansing; for Muslims, *wudu*, the ritual washing that must take place before prayer.

Whatever the intent, it is evident that the bath is a significant part of our history.

Renewal

A BATH IS NEVER ORDINARY. Baths are different every day of your life because you are different. Change one element: aromatherapy, candles, soap, music, silence. Use what you need for that particular bath to make it unique. Take a bath in candlelight or completely in the dark. Start at the top of your head and work to your toes relaxing yourself in the water. Run a bubble bath and play sculptor with the foam.

The bath is also a great place to meditate and do guided imagery. You can let your mind take you to any place in the universe. What a wonderful gift to combine the healing power of the bath, with the healing power of guided imagery.

The bath is an act of re-creation and re-membering. *Re-membering* the waters of your mother's womb. *Recreating* what you need today. *Releasing*: write in the water any experience or emotion you want to release from your body or soul. These words take presence in the water. As you open the drain, imagine the words swirling down the drain. *Reclaim* who you are, uncluttered, focused, and new. The bath is an opportunity to respond to the holy.

When you bathe, you are engaging in a time honored sacred ritual.

Prayer and Contemplation

---

*"Every major religion has referred
to inner guidance in its teachings…
the Spirit of Christ, the Atman,
God within…"*—CHRISTINE M. COMSTOCK

PRAYER MAKES US AWARE of the presence of God. There are many paths into that divine presence. Human beings have spent centuries and lifetimes exploring avenues to get closer to God. Each of us wants the full experience of Divine love, acceptance, and communion. We have attempted this within ourselves and across cultures with many types of prayers.

Many convincing studies demonstrate prayer does effect healing. Dr. Larry Dossey, a physician, has become a leading authority in the newly emerging field of healing and prayer. Dr. Dossey cites hundreds of studies that verify the effectiveness of prayer in the healing process. Cardiologist Randolph Byrd at San Francisco General Hospital took 393 patients admitted to the coronary care unit and divided them into two groups. One group had 192 patients that were prayed for by home prayer groups of five to seven people. The second group was 201 patients that were not remembered in prayer. The study was conducted with strict criteria. Neither the doctors, nurses, nor patients, knew which group individual patients were in. The study concluded the prayed-for patients were five times less likely than the non-prayed-for group to require antibiotics. They were three times less likely to develop pulmonary edema. None of the prayed-for patients needed endotracheal intubations. Fewer patients in the prayed-for group died. The scientific literature that substantiates prayer and healing grows by the day.

The federal government's new Office of Alternative Medicine reports that for over 25 years Dr. Herbert Benson at Harvard has created a large body of research on the science of meditation. The research demonstrates meditation also improves health. According to many years of research we know people who meditate have significantly fewer migraine headaches, their anxiety and depression levels drop remarkably, employees miss fewer days at work, most patients with high blood pressure recover completely, or at least improve, and 75 percent of insomniacs are cured and 25 percent improve. The healing effects of meditation have gained scientific acceptance.

Catherine of Sienna wrote: "Perfect prayer is achieved, not with many words, but with loving desire. Everything you do can be a prayer." Prayer has usually been taught as a discipline that must be learned, but nothing could be further from the truth. Prayer is as natural as our breathing. It is natural for us to want to be in a relationship with the Divine. It merely takes having the intention to be aware of the Divine presence in all things.

There are many manners of prayer. A prayer of petition is asking something for one's self. Intercessory prayer is asking something for others—be it healing, forgiveness, or guidance. We offer gratitude in a prayer of thanksgiving. Centering prayer—an ancient form of Christian contemplative prayer—involves entering silence and listening to God. The examination of conscience is a type of prayer where we conduct a moral inventory of our lives, examining ourselves, and thereby developing an honesty with ourselves and with God. The final stage of the prayer of examen is asking for forgiveness. The types of prayer shift within traditions and continue to evolve with new approaches.

Cycles of Prayer

AS VARIED AS THE TYPES OF PRAYER are the cycles of prayer. We have annual cycles of prayer that differ according to spiritual and religious traditions. For Christians, the Lenten prayers are prayers of forgiveness. For Jews, the prayers of Yom Kippur are prayers of repentance. For Muslims, the prayers of Ramadan are prayers of sacrifice and devotion. Different traditions have daily cycles of prayer. Muslims are required by the practice of *salat*—to pray five times a day. Jews pray three times daily, each time designated by one of the founders of the faith. Christians are reminded to pray upon waking, before meals, and before going to sleep.

Religions have developed not only many methods for prayer, but also many aids to assist us in the practice of prayer. Many spiritual practitioners use prayer beads, which are found in almost every major religion. Prayer rugs are used in Islam to keep the site of prayer free from dirt of any sort. Prayer flags are used by Tibetan Buddhists to carry prayers and blessings to all the people in the path of the wind. Icons—painted images of Christ or holy people—are physical objects to help connect you to God. *Mezuzahs* hold a prayer of blessing at the door of the Jewish home.

How to Pray

PRAYER IS THE MOST PERSONAL and intimate of all spiritual practices. Different types of prayer resonate with different types of people. Explore different methods of prayer for yourself. In the centering prayer—the ancient practice of contemplation—you sit in a quite place, focus on your breath, and then repeat one word or a small phrase over and over, eventually experiencing communion with God. Many people prefer a memorized prayer like the Christian "The Lord's Prayer." You can also pray with holy scriptures. Meditation varies as well, but the most basic form is going into silence and listening.

Prayer is about first becoming aware then discovering God in that awareness. A saint from the early Christian church said it this way:

> "Help us find God," the disciples asked the elder.
> "No one can help you do that," the elder said.

"Why not?" the disciples asked, amazed.

"For the same reason that no one can help fish to find the ocean."

Sleeping

---

*"Blessings on him that first invented sleep!
It covers a man thoughts and all, like a cloak;
it is meat for the hungry, drink for the thirsty,
heat for the cold, and cold for the hot. It is the
current coin that purchases cheaply all the
pleasures of the world, and the balance that sets
even king and shepherd, fool and sage."*
—CERVANTES

WE ARE, AS A NATION, in danger because of our lack of reverence for sleep. Sleep is not a luxury, it is a necessity, yet over 100 million Americans are sleep deprived. Sleep should be a naturally occurring cycle instead of something we continually try to manage and control. Just as the seasons and other aspects of nature manifest cycles, sleep is a natural, cyclical event that we must honor.

Part of the modern problem with lack of sleep is over stimulation. With the advent of late night shows, thousands of channels to surf, all-night social events, even round-the-clock, fully-lit sporting venues, we have trouble going to sleep.

America is running on six hours of sleep or less. Over-the-counter sleeping pills are one of the fastest growing categories of medicine. Insomnia has become an epidemic. Still, people do not want to go to their doctors about this problem. Sleep aids may offer a temporary fix, but they are not solving the problem as they do not treat the underlying cause.

Treating the physiological component won't work especially if it is a spiritual problem. The precise function of sleep remains a mystery, but as we spend one-third of our lives sleeping, doesn't it deserve our respect?

Sleep Science

THERE ARE IMMEASURABLE HEALTH IMPLICATIONS for lack of sleep. You can have significant mood shifts, including depression and increased irritability. You may lose coping skills. You can experience more stress and anxiety. You may experience weight gain, because the anxiety of sleep deprivation can cause you to eat more. Without sleep, your body's immune cells don't function. Consequently, your immunity to infections and disease is reduced. Your productivity is reduced because your cognitive functioning is impaired.

Approximately one-third of all drivers have fallen asleep at some point while driving a car.

We must have sleep: It is a matter of life and death. Our bodies must have deep, REM sleep to function. We must have this REM sleep. We must dream to maintain us emotionally, physically, and spiritually. You can very literally go insane without REM sleep. What's more, sleep is an essential component for a meaningful life.

Sleep Tight

SLEEP SHOULD BE EXPERIENCED as renewal. It is a biological, restorative function. Every system in your body is refreshed each time you sleep.

Listen to your body. Be aware of your body. Your body will tell you how much sleep you need. Practice awareness and tend to your soul's needs. Imagine sleep as grace. Surrender. Allow yourself to be enveloped with sleep's grace, its abundance, caring, and healing nature.

Invest in your bedroom by adding peaceful colors, a good mattress, nice sheets, a comfortable pillow. It is worth it. You spend a third of your life there. Treat yourself by creating a reverent space that honors sleep for the holy and sacred experience that it is.

A Bird Named Goober

WHAT IS HOLDING YOU BACK from living a meaningful and intentional life? Are you ready to confront, as Thoreau put it, "the essential facts of life?"

For me, a dirty bathroom was an opportunity to move beyond judgment and rage. Removing a dead dog from the road taught me reverence and respect for all God's creations. Experiencing political defeat offered lessons in humility and in the healing, transformational power of community. The split second of an accident crystallized the realization that we are all one human family.

Any misfortune might call forth the courage and compassion that has been long hidden within you. But your own journey is not likely to, nor should it, begin with such dramatic events. It takes practice. You can do it, not through ritual or dogma or elaborate schemes, but merely through awareness and intention.

I hope this book has helped you see the many opportunities to turn everyday events into spiritually rewarding experiences. That it has provided inspiration to surrender to those moments. Before long, the idea of living beyond your comfort zone will be welcomed, not feared. Paths less taken will provide the deep sense of satisfaction and peace of mind you crave in our complex, noisy, and careless modern world.

I WAS HUNTING FOR A TABLE at The Flying Biscuit, a popular restaurant in Atlanta that I often frequent. I was number thirty in line and the hostess had just called out number five. My daughter was late meeting me, so with unexpected time on my hands I wandered down the street. All of a sudden, the sky opened up and it poured. I ducked into a little gift shop.

It was an adorable shop filled with pottery and unusual gifts. Pre-occupied with my thoughts, I browsed around with little interest, occasionally picking something up and putting it down.

Something screeched. I looked around but didn't see anything. I picked up a teapot and heard the sound again. I noticed the shopkeeper was unpacking some pottery by the cash register. She seemed unaffected by the weird noise.

I approached the woman and looked behind the counter. There was an old bird cage on the floor with a tiny bird inside gazing up at me. The shopkeeper noticed my inquisitiveness, walked over and lifted the cage onto the counter.

She smiled and said, "This is Goober. He's crying because it's time for his lunch." As she opened the cage, she said, "Don't worry. He can't fly away. His wing is broken." She then opened a small plastic container and picked up a single chopstick. She picked up a tiny bit of food with the chopstick and slowly and reverently fed the obviously weak creature.

She looked over to me. "People race up and down the road outside. They hit these little birds and occasionally a cat or a dog. I don't have much money. I have a few health problems myself. But this is something good I can do in the world. No one else seems to care about these little critters. I believe they are all really angels sent here to love us."

Such a beautiful awareness. She had seen a need, surrendered to create a spiritual practice. She rescued tiny creatures that others don't see and mostly don't care about.

I was deeply moved by the tenderness with which she fed Goober. Her movements were mindful and holy. I stayed for over an hour and watched in amazement. I was humbled to be in the presence of the woman and her pet. She explained to me that she goes home at night and with her arthritic hands, cuts, peels, mashes, and then (with great intention, I was sure) mixes grapes, seeds, and honey for the birds. She believed that her devotion goes into the little bird's food and that will help him get better.

I was awed by her reverence: by her awareness of this small, ordinary animal. Mother Teresa is surely right. The secret is doing small things with great love.

SO BEGIN WITH GREAT LOVE in your heart and a small thing in your life. You will not stumble over the divine, but you can discover it: in surprising places, in fleeting moments, in the simplest of ways. It can be found every day, and transformation is the reward.